CHICAGO BEARS

YESTERDAY & TODAY ™

JEFF DAVIS
FOREWORD BY GARY FENCIK

WEST
SIDE
PUBLISHING

Jeff Davis has been a writer, as well as a producer for television news, sports, and documentaries—earning five Emmy Awards for outstanding programs—since he completed active duty as a U.S. Navy lieutenant in 1967. Davis has written two acclaimed biographies: *Papa Bear: The Life and Legacy of George Halas* and *Rozelle: Czar of the NFL.* His new novel, *Smoke Rings,* is set in suburban Chicago in the mid-20th century. He and his wife, Kirsten, live in Evanston, Illinois; they have two children and two grandchildren.

Contributing writer **John Crist** is the publisher of *Bear Report* magazine, a monthly publication dedicated solely to coverage of the Chicago Bears.

Gary Fencik played 12 seasons with the Chicago Bears and is their all-time leader in interceptions and total takeaways. In addition to making several Pro Bowl and All NFL teams during his career, he also won a gold record and platinum video award for 1985's *The Super Bowl Shuffle.*

Facts verified by Roy Taylor.

Front cover photos (left to right): Walter Payton, Dick Butkus, Mike Ditka, Bronko Nagurski, Brian Urlacher

Back cover photos (left to right): Harold "Red" Grange, Gale Sayers, George Halas, Sid Luckman

Yesterday & Today is a trademark of Publications International, Ltd.

West Side Publishing is a division of Publications International, Ltd.

Louis Weber, CEO
Publications International, Ltd.
7373 North Cicero Avenue
Lincolnwood, Illinois 60712

Permission is never granted for commercial purposes.

ISBN-13: 978-1-4127-6117-8
ISBN-10: 1-4127-6117-4

Manufactured in China.

8 7 6 5 4 3 2 1

Library of Congress Control Number: 2009923895

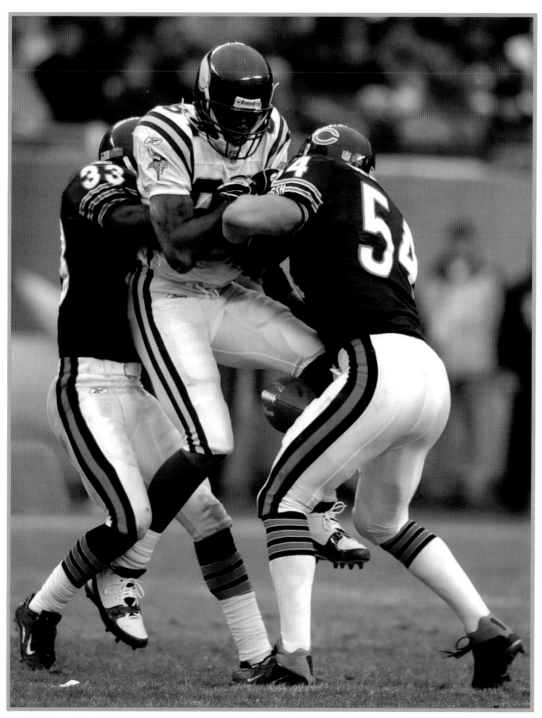

Minnesota Vikings Randy Moss drops the ball after a hit by Chicago Bears Brian Urlacher (54) and Charles Tillman (33) on December 14, 2003, at Soldier Field. The Bears won 13–10.

CONTENTS

George Halas

1925 Game Program

Dick Butkus

Modern Pennant

CHAPTER FOUR
THE AGE OF IRON MIKE

CHAPTER FIVE
THE MODERN ERA

CHAPTER SIX

Walter Payton

Devin Hester Bobblehead

Brian Urlacher

FOREWORD
BY GARY FENCIK

There are very few players in the NFL who are fortunate enough to play for their hometown team as I did for 12 years with the Chicago Bears. I progressed from watching the Bears play at Wrigley Field on television when I was a kid to playing with Walter Payton, who was the only starting running back I played with for 12 consecutive seasons! I had three coaches during that tenure—Jack Pardee, Neill Armstrong, and Mike Ditka. I remember the first time Mike Ditka addressed our team in the spring of 1982 to discuss the priorities of the Chicago Bears. Mike was the first coach to state in plain terms that our goal was not just to win the NFL Central Division or the NFC, our goal was to get to and win the Super Bowl. The bad news, he said, was that half of us wouldn't be there when we finally reached our goal. When I looked at the game program in the locker room as we prepared for Super Bowl XX, I realized Ditka was right, only about one third of the team that heard his original speech was present as we prepared to take on the New England Patriots for the biggest game of my life. Since my retirement, I've had the pleasure of going to games with my son Garrison and recognizing the incredible impact the game has on fans each Sunday.

Gary Fencik

Being born and raised in Chicago as a Bears fan has given me a unique perspective on just how passionate fans are about this team and the special relationship players have with fans of this founding NFL franchise. As a kid, I remember when the Bears' preseason games were tape-delayed while Jack Brickhouse provided the radio play-by-play for players such as Billy Wade, Ronnie Bull, or Dick Gordon. But the two players that defined the game were Gayle Sayers and Dick Butkus. It's still hard to imagine having two first-round picks and future Hall of Famers who have shaped the definition of "great" in their respective positions but neither ever played in a postseason game.

As a player, I began to meet many of the players I idolized as a kid. And this makes you begin to appreciate being a part of a very special franchise. When you put on the dark blue home jersey of the Chicago Bears, you are connected to one of the great traditions in professional football. You also realize, as you will read in the stories in this book, how far the game of football has progressed. While new stadiums have dramatically improved the experience of attending a game, we owe a great deal to the former players whose contributions and commitment to football have made it what it is today. In this sense, these stories unify the common experience we all feel for the Chicago Bears regardless of the year or the team's record.

I always wondered how difficult it was to play a football game at Wrigley Field, where the north end zone ended with the brick wall in left field. It wasn't until I discussed this with Ronnie Bull, Mike Pyle, and other former Bears that I realized the left field end zone was the good one—the south end zone sloped and went into what is today the visitor's dugout at Wrigley Field. Virginia McCaskey told me that as a young girl she remembered Dick Plasman, the last NFL player to play

National Football League

Go Bears' Gary Fencik 45

without a helmet, being taken off on a stretcher after falling into the dugout following a catch. I mistakenly thought she was referring to leather versus plastic helmets. Can you imagine: This guy literally played with no protection at all! Now that is tough.

Near the end of the 1981 season, it became pretty clear that we would be facing a potential coaching change; Alan Page and I wrote a letter to George Halas asking him to consider retaining Buddy Ryan and the defensive coaches if head coach Neill Armstrong was fired. We had each defensive player sign the letter, and on a snowy December afternoon, George Halas came to our practice at the U.S. Navy Great Lakes training center (we didn't have an indoor practice facility) and told the defensive players that our coaches would be back the following year. I don't think most Bear fans realize Mike Ditka inherited, rather than hired, Buddy Ryan as his coach and this, in part, led to the creative tension that existed between Buddy and Mike until Buddy's departure following the Super Bowl in 1985. It was a great honor to have been a part of the 1985 Super Bowl team, and almost 25 years later, that team continues to have a very special place in every Bear fan I meet.

Sitting in the stands for the last 20 years has given me yet another perspective on how emotionally involved fans are with this team. Good or bad, through Wannie and Jauron and now Lovie, fans are so emotionally involved in each game. I've watched some really good players, including Urlacher, Brown, and Briggs, who could play on any team in any era. I hope the reader comes away from this book with a greater appreciation of the important role the Chicago Bears franchise has played in making the game what it is today and appreciates how much fun every guy who has worn a Bears uniform has had playing in Chicago. Go Bears!

Gary Fencik

Gary Fencik

Above left: *This commemorative NFL football is signed by Gary Fencik, number 45.* **Above:** *Fencik was a free safety with the Bears and is their all-time leader in interceptions and total tackles.*

CHAPTER ONE

THE BEARS' BEGINNING

1920–1939

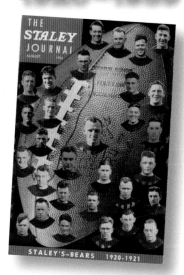

"George, I know you like football better than starch.... Why don't you take the football team to Chicago. I think football will go over big there!"

A. E. STALEY TO GEORGE HALAS, 1921

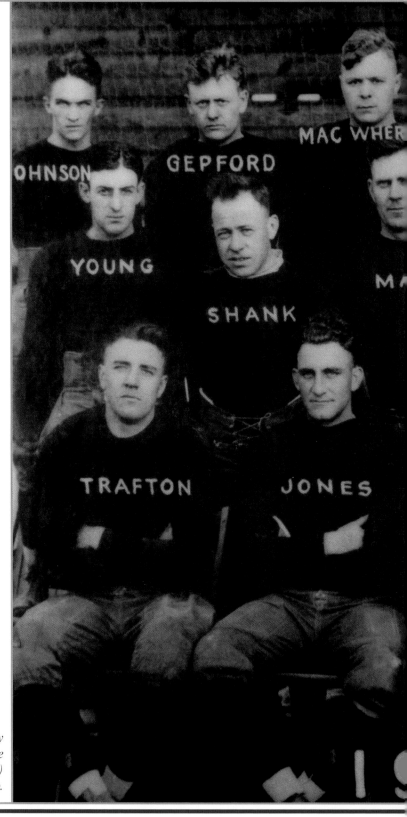

Above: *The 1956* Staley Journal, *issued by the A. E. Staley company, features the 1920 Staley team.* **Right:** *In 1920, the Decatur Staleys were one of the NFL's first franchise teams. George Halas (front row, middle) organized the team, and Ed Sternaman (top row, second from right) became his partner in 1921, when the team moved from Decatur to Chicago.*

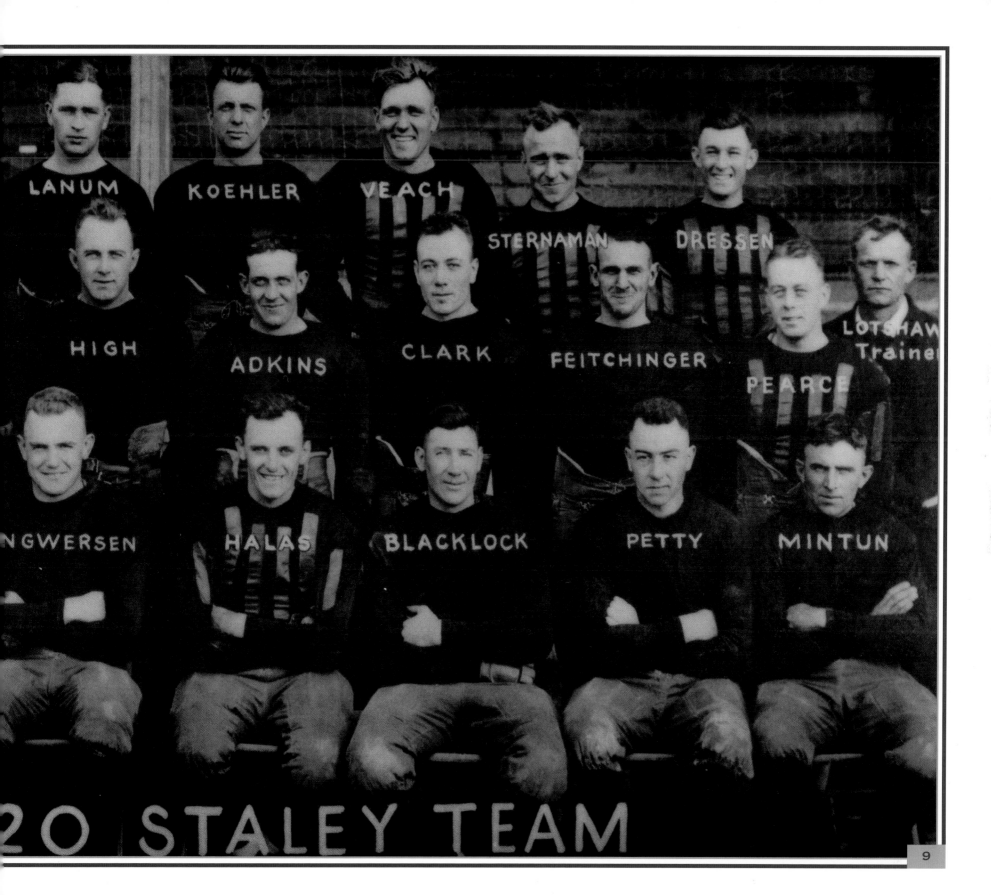

LANUM　KOEHLER　VEACH　STERNAMAN　DRESSEN

HIGH　ADKINS　CLARK　FEITCHINGER　PEARCE　LOTSHAW Trainer

NGWERSEN　HALAS　BLACKLOCK　PETTY　MINTUN

20 STALEY TEAM

BEAT THE (CORN) STARCH OUT OF THE OTHER GUY

Owner of the Decatur, Illinois-based corn-products company, A. E. Staley believed that company-sponsored teams increased product sales and boosted employee morale. In March 1920, he sent aide George Chamberlain to Chicago to hire a young George Halas to organize, recruit, and coach a winning, company-sponsored football team. Staley took action after the University of Illinois athletic director, George Huff, and football coach, Bob Zuppke, strongly endorsed Halas, their former three-sport star in football, baseball, and basketball. The 25-year-old Halas, a civil engineer who was designing bridges for the Chicago, Burlington and Quincy Railroad, was recruited to supervise starch production but also to play baseball in the spring and summer and become Staley's athletic director, assembling a football team to beat the starch out of opponents on Sundays in the fall.

Halas, in turn, told Staley he needed his support in order to recruit top-quality former college and service players: These players would need the offer of a steady, year-round job and a share in gate receipts. Staley agreed, and Halas landed many of the finest players in the Midwest. The best was center-

Red Grange launches a pass in the 19–7 Bears win over the Giants before a record pro football crowd of 73,000. Grange gained 128 yards and scored on a 35-yard pass play in the biggest game in early league history at the Polo Grounds in New York on December 6, 1925.

linebacker George "The Beast" (or "Brute") Trafton; he was signed after being kicked off the Notre Dame team by Knute Rockne in 1919 for playing semi-pro games under an assumed name. Trafton, who Red Grange called the toughest, most ornery cuss he ever met, played 13 years for the Bears and was elected to the Pro Football Hall of Fame in 1964.

From their start in 1920, Halas and the Decatur Staleys dominated the league, as the Chicago Bears would for many years to follow. They beat the Moline Tractors (a non-league team) 20–0 on October 3 in the season opener in Decatur, beginning a ten-game unbeaten streak as they made their way through small cites in Illinois, Indiana, and Minnesota. This trek eventually led them to the league's first Thanksgiving Day game on November 25 on Chicago's North Side against the hometown Tigers; the Staleys beat them 6–0. It was the team's first game at Cubs Park—the future Wrigley Field that was to be their playing ground for the next half century. When Halas saw the crowd of 8,000 fans, he knew this ballpark, in his hometown, was the place he wanted the team to call home.

The Bears (on defense) beat the Columbus Tigers 14–13 on November 29, 1925, at Cubs Park. It was only the second game in the Red Grange tour—the Bears traveled all over the country, playing 19 games in 2 months and popularizing pro football.

A LEAGUE FOR LOVE, LITTLE MONEY

Before the Staleys' first game, George Halas took the train from Decatur to Canton, Ohio, for a September 17, 1920, meeting with other team owners. They came from other cities in Ohio, including Akron, Cleveland, Dayton, and Massillon, as well as Rochester, New York; Muncie and Hammond, Indiana; Chicago and Rock Island, Illinois; and Racine, Wisconsin. In a sweltering Hupmobile auto showroom, the owners formed the American Professional Football Association (APFA). The charter fee was $100, but as Halas later admitted, no money changed hands because no one had any. Because the association was organized so late, scheduling for the 1920 season was haphazard. Furthermore, Commissioner Jim Thorpe was a rather inept figurehead—no one kept records, and no one could crown a formal champion. Fortunately, the APFA had a single visionary determined to see the league through to success, no matter how long it would take: George Halas.

The following Sunday, at Normal Park on Chicago's South Side, the Chicago Cardinals beat the Staleys 7–6 on a disputed late touchdown. Accounts vary, but there is one claim that a Cardinal receiver caught a pass near the sideline, cut behind the crowd, using it for interference, and scored. Fearing for his life if he called the Cardinal out of bounds, the referee swallowed his whistle. However, the Staleys beat the Cardinals 10–0 in a December 5 rematch at Cubs Park. A week later, the Staleys played the Akron Pros, with their African American star Fritz Pollard (who was from Chicago's Rogers Park neighborhood), in a hastily arranged championship game. Before a crowd of 12,000 at Cubs Park, the largest yet to see a league game, the teams played to a scoreless tie that left the Staleys at 10–1–2 and Akron at 8–0–3.

Over Halas's vehement protests, the Ohio-based and influenced Association teams (a group of professional football teams that banded together to form a national league) awarded the championship to Akron the following April. Halas vowed revenge but soon would gain redemption. In true fashion, though, Papa Bear seethed over that "lost title," maintaining that his team had a rightful claim to it.

PAPA BEAR

George Stanley Halas was born on Chicago's West Side on February 2, 1895, to Czech immigrants Frank and Barbara Poledna Halas. His parents instilled in him the value of hard work, as well as the drive to excel.

Halas gained his love for athletics at his high school, Crane Tech. At Crane, he also developed a lifelong friendship with fellow west-sider Ralph Brizzolara. At key moments in their long friendship, Brizzolara came to the aid of his friend. He extended money to the team—a $5,000 loan in 1932 helped save the Bears franchise. Brizzolara ran the team during World War II while Papa Bear served in the Pacific. In 1947, Brizzolara designed the bleachers that covered the outfield and increased Wrigley Field's capacity to nearly 50,000 during football season. He also served as club secretary.

While in high school, Halas met Min Bushing. Brizzolara served as best man when Halas married Min in 1922. By 1925, George and Min had two children: Virginia and George Jr., nicknamed "Mugs." They would both play prominent roles

Red Grange (third from left) and George Halas (middle) pictured at Cubs Park in December 1925, before the Bears board a train to begin their long football journey. They played ten games in the next month on the Eastern phase of the national tour.

in the franchise during the later years as Halas built the Bears and the league.

At the University of Illinois, Halas starred on the Illini football, basketball, and baseball teams, earning a degree in civil engineering in 1918. Later that spring, at Great Lakes Naval Training Station, he received a U.S. Naval Reserve commission. But instead of joining the fleet, Ensign Halas joined the Great Lakes football team, where, on New Year's Day 1919, he was named Player of the Rose Bowl as Great Lakes beat the Mare Island Marines 17–0.

Halas was just 25 years old when he founded his team and the league in 1920. For the next 63 years, until his death

At the Los Angeles Coliseum on November 2, 1958, George Halas surveys the largest crowd (100,470) to watch a Bears game—it was the second largest crowd in NFL history. Unfortunately, the Rams beat the Bears 41–35, and the 8–4 Bears finished second in the NFL West behind the Baltimore Colts.

HAIL TO THE ORANGE, NAVY BLUE, AND WHITE

Out of fidelity to his alma mater, the University of Illinois, and after lyrics from the school song, "Illinois Loyalty," George Halas chose orange and blue as the Bears team colors in 1920. In their startup season in Decatur and during the early Chicago years, the Staleys wore blue jerseys with vertical tan leather stripes—orange in appearance—that helped runners and receivers grip the slippery, oblong ball.

True to form, Halas, the forward-thinker and inveterate tinkerer, eventually amended the color scheme. To honor his Navy service, he changed the darker hue from Illini blue to navy blue and added white, but he retained the orange shade of the Illini. The navy blue was closer to the naval officer's service dress "blue" uniform for years. It appeared to be black to most observers and still looks that way from a distance on cloudy or rainy days.

Captain Harold "Red" Grange—late in his final collegiate season (1925)—leads his Fighting Illini teammates out of the locker room at Illinois Memorial Stadium before the kickoff of a game against the University of Chicago.

was most proud of the time he recovered a Jim Thorpe fumble in a 1923 game at Cubs Park against Canton and, with Thorpe in hot pursuit, weaved and sprinted for his life (as he put it) for a 98-yard touchdown—the longest fumble recovery return in NFL history for decades.

Halas led the NFL through its infancy in the 1920s, kept it alive in the Depression, guided it through World War II while serving with Admiral Chester Nimitz in the Pacific, and returned to lead it through two pro football wars and merger settlements, the last in the '60s. In 1960, he cast the deciding vote in the league meeting to elect young visionary Pete Rozelle as commissioner. Until Rozelle, Halas had to obtain frequent off-season loans to keep his franchise afloat until season-ticket money arrived each spring. Halas was also first to understand that television would sell his league to the masses—this enterprise made him and his fellow owners part of the richest and most powerful sports organization on earth.

Essentially, Halas was a godfather figure—the Papa Bear. As Red Grange loved to tell it, "George recruited and signed the players, managed the money, wrote the press releases, sold the tickets, coached and won more games than anybody else, and wrote most of the league rules."

This is young George Halas in 1925. In his thirties, he was the Bears' right end, as well as the team's co-owner, co-head coach, publicity agent, and ticket manager. He ran the Bears in his image until his death in 1983, 63 years after he founded the team and the league.

on October 31, 1983, Halas owned the Bears, coached in 40 seasons, and was the National Football League's dominant figure. With Halas as head coach in four ten-year hitches from 1920 to 1967, the Bears won 324 games, a record that lasted until Miami's Don Shula surpassed it in 1993. Halas won his first title in 1921 when Warren Harding was president and his NFL-record sixth title in 1963 when Lyndon Johnson was chief executive. Halas was named Coach of the Year twice: in 1963 at age 68 and again two years later. As a player, Halas

This football proudly states which team started the business of pro football in 1920.

Howard Barry did a pre-game, advance story in the *Chicago Tribune* on October 16, 1930, on the professional debut of Bronko Nagurski with the Bears.

Hail Bronko Nagurski—He's an Old Fashioned He-Man

BY HOWARD BARRY.

Bronko Nagurski—the radio announcers always liked to roll it off their tongues. People listening from their warm living rooms caught the image of a rugged he-man from way up where the wilderness begins charging across the chalk lines of a wind swept Minnesota gridiron.

Now Bronko lives in a steam heated apartment over on Pine Grove avenue and spends his afternoons reading books or going to picture shows. But don't think he's domesticated yet. Those who watch the Bears and Cardinals play next Sunday are quite likely to see the Bronko Nagurski who is all that his name implies—Bronko Nagurski, who proved last fall at Dyche stadium that the twilight of the strong men was not yet at hand.

No Subs for Bronko.

Before that game between Minnesota and Northwestern followers of football had been pointing out that in the old days a fellow went in there and played from the first whistle until the last, unless he was carried off beforehand. But with the development of shock troops and the practice of making wholesale substitutions football players were said to be losing their virility and becoming a race of softies. Then came the Gophers and Bronko Nagurski. Newspaper accounts Minnesota's greater

New on Pro Grid

BRONKO NAGURSKI.

pressed a shudder, because Bronko Nagurski is no man to be putting all his weight on the hind legs of any chair. He's well over six feet and is built in proportion, with powerful shoulders and a neck like a battering

This is the program for the first pro football championship game from December 1920, between the Staleys and the Akron Pros.

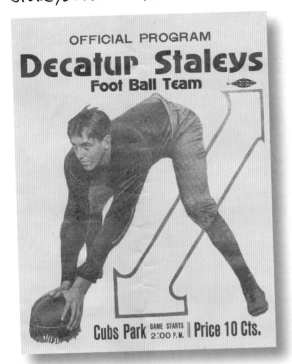

OFFICIAL PROGRAM
Decatur Staleys
Foot Ball Team
Cubs Park GAME STARTS 2:00 P.M. | Price 10 Cts.

FOOTBALL

Chicago Bears
with
RED GRANGE — BRONKO NAGURSKI
DICK NESBITT — HERB JOESTING
vs.
Cleveland Panthers
with
LEO RASKOWSKI, Ohio State
KEN HOUSER, W. & J.
HOWARD KRISS, Ohio State

SUNDAY 2:30 P.M.
September 18th

TICKETS ON SALE AT
A. G. SPALDING'S   211 South State Street
BEARS' HEADQUARTERS   453 Conway Building
                                    Phone Franklin 6040

Loyola Stadium
LOYOLA AVE. AT SHERIDAN ROAD
Take North Side "L" to Loyola Station

RED GRANGE

BOX SEATS
$1.65

GENERAL ADMISSION
$1.10

CHILDREN UNDER 16
40 Cents

This poster promotes an exhibition game at Loyola University in 1932: the Bears versus the semi-pro Cleveland Panthers. The main attractions were Bears' stars Red Grange and Bronko Nagurski.

In 1922, this was a ticket holder's season pass; it allowed entry into any home game during the season.

Chicago Bears
Football Club
TENDERS TO
1922 PASS
Mr. Geo. _____
THE COURTESY OF THE Cubs Park
No. 38
EDW. C. STERNAMAN
GEO. S. HALAS

Red Grange returned to the Bears in 1929 after forming his own league failed. Hampered by a knee injury, he was still a star and a poster boy for the team.

Red Grange lines up at fullback as the Bears scrimmage with a junior team at Wrigley Field in 1934. The Bears sponsored Chicago Park District football teams for years.

Bronko Nagurski, at 6'2", 230 pounds, was a human stick of dynamite. George Halas called him the greatest football player who ever lived. Nagurski was a charter Hall of Famer, as well as a pro wrestler, as can be seen from his stance.

Bronko Nagurski leaps over his fellow teammates in practice. Red Grange compared Nagurski's hitting and tackling ability, along with his defensive fierceness, to Dick Butkus.

SWEET HOME CHICAGO

The young APFA had a momentous season in 1921. Because the league did not honor his 1920 title claim, Halas engineered an April coup to replace league president Jim Thorpe with experienced athletic administrator Joe Carr of Columbus, Ohio.

A month later, when the economy turned sour, Staley told Halas he wanted him to take over the team, then move it to Chicago—where Halas always wanted to be anyway. He then handed Halas a $5,000 check to make it worth his while. For Halas's side of the bargain, he was obligated to retain the Staley name for the balance of the 1921 season.

To share costs, Halas made what he always called the worst deal of his life. He invited Ed "Dutch" Sternaman, his friend and teammate going back to their Illinois days, to be his equal partner. This 50/50 arrangement worked in the beginning, but it would fall apart by the end of the decade, nearly costing Halas his team.

At the August league meeting, Halas allowed the Green Bay Packers (who were community-owned) to join; young Notre Dame dropout Earl "Curly" Lambeau was their coach at the time. In the November 27, 1921, inaugural game at Cubs Park, the Staleys kicked off pro football's greatest rivalry with a 20–0 victory; Halas scored one of three touchdowns.

Another deal that could have changed everything went awry that fall. In need of a marquee-gate attraction, Halas signed a letter of agreement with Ohio State's Chic Harley, a star so bright that people in Columbus still call the 105,000-seat Ohio Stadium "The House That Harley Built." When Harley and his brother demanded that Halas and Sternaman award them a third of the club, Halas cut Chic Harley five games into the

season. The Harleys sued, but Halas won every point in court the following spring.

Halas, the businessman in the partnership, cut a rental agreement with Chicago Cubs president William L. Veeck Sr. In return for use of Cubs Park for practice and games, Halas agreed to pay the ballclub 15 percent of the gate receipts, plus the concessions. Veeck let Halas keep the proceeds from program sales. That handshake deal lasted 50 years.

The Staleys went 9–1–1 to beat Buffalo by a half game, winning the first sanctioned APFA championship. It was the start of something big, and Halas and Sternaman closed the books on a successful season that saw them end up with seven dollars in the bank.

Left: *Manager Charles C. "Cash and Carry" Pyle was the catalyst behind Red Grange's Hollywood career. Grange starred in a few silent films in the late 1920s.* Above: *An exhausted Red Grange gets a break from one of the 19 games he played during the two-month tour. C. C. Pyle watches over Grange—his meal ticket. They each made $300,000 from the tour.*

WE ARE THE BEARS

As a boy, George Halas was a baseball hopeful and a rabid Cubs fan. A star football end, basketball guard, and baseball outfielder at Illinois, Halas drew his Navy discharge in early 1919, just in time to join the New York Yankees, where manager Miller Huggins installed the speedy, switch-hitting Chicagoan in right field.

Three interlocking events ended Halas's baseball career after a dozen big-league games. He lost his speed when he injured a hip in a spring training slide. He could not hit a curveball and thus was sent to the minors. Then, in the 1919 off-season, the Yankees acquired a right fielder, also named George, who could hit everything: George Herman "Babe" Ruth.

Halas may have left playing professional baseball behind, but he never forgot the scores of Cubs games he attended as a boy at the old West Side Park. After the 1921 season, when Halas was free to change the team name from the Decatur Staleys, it wasn't hard for him to come up with something related to his baseball past: Because a Bear is the nasty big

In the early years, George Halas tried everything to promote the Bears. He wrote the press releases, sold the tickets, and hired the owner of this decked out roadster to plug the 1925 home opener against the defending NFL champions, the Cleveland Bulldogs.

brother to the smaller and milder Cub, and the team played at Cubs Park, Halas decided that "Bears" would be the team's new moniker.

On May 22, 1922, Halas and partner Ed Sternaman formally incorporated the team as the Chicago Bears Football Club, with a capital value of $15,000. Each man put up $2,500 and then made another $2,500 joint contribution to give the team $7,500 in working capital. The remaining $7,500 consisted of unfunded stock certificates, which they locked in a safe.

The '22 Bears finished second in defense of their title but gained a future Hall of Famer in pro football's first trade. When the Rock Island Independents failed to pay the Bears $100 in gate receipts, Halas claimed their star tackle, Ed Healey, in lieu of the payment. When Healey died many years later on December 19, 1978, Halas ordered public address announcer Chet Coppock to tell the Soldier Field crowd, "We regretfully must inform you that Ed Healey, the greatest offensive tackle in Bears history, passed away today."

EXIT APFA, ENTER NFL

From the beginning, George Halas just didn't like the name American Professional Football Association. He thought it sounded minor league and second rate. Thus, in a June 1922 meeting that saved the financially troubled Green Bay Packers franchise from disbanding, Halas stood up and told his fellow owners that their league needed a new, better name. "We are first class," he said.

Because Halas was now the Papa Bear playing in the baseball home of his favorite ballclub, the National League's Chicago Cubs, he said it should be called the National "Football" League. "My fellow members agreed," Halas wrote decades later. And so the name stuck: National Football League, or NFL.

THE GALLOPING GHOST

In the orange luminescence of the dedication game on October 18, 1924, at a packed Illinois Memorial Stadium, Harold "Red" Grange burst into football immortality. In the opening 12 minutes of play against the Illini's bitter rival, Michigan, Grange scored on four long touchdown runs and gained 363 all-purpose yards. It stands as the most spectacular performance in football history; Illinois routed Michigan 39–14 as Grange scored five touchdowns and passed for a sixth to total 402 yards. Although sports writer Grantland Rice was covering Notre Dame's Four Horsemen in their epic win over Army that day in New York, he rebounded a few days later to coin football's most enduring nickname, calling Grange "The Galloping Ghost."

George Halas first saw Grange in action in November 1924, when the redhead totaled 186 yards as Illinois crushed Iowa 36–0 at Memorial Stadium. At last, Halas found the marquee player who would take the National Football League into the big time.

He pursued Grange thereafter but had to work through Champaign movie theater proprietor and outrageous promoter Charles C. "Cash and Carry" Pyle. Halas started negotiating with Pyle, who was Grange's manager, late in Illinois's 1925 season. After Grange played his final

Red Grange returned to the Bears and the NFL in 1929 after he tried to form his own league and failed. Hampered by a knee injury, he was still an all-around star.

Red Grange takes off on a 67-yard touchdown run—his second of five touchdowns as Illinois routs Michigan 39–14 at the Illinois Memorial Stadium Dedication Game in Champaign on October 18, 1924, in football's greatest-ever performance.

game at Ohio State, Pyle hustled him to Chicago, where he signed an unprecedented guaranteed $100,000 contract with Halas. Grange and Pyle would bank another $200,000 on the grueling barnstorming tour billed as "Red Grange, George Halas, and the Chicago Bears." The Bears got half the proceeds. Grange and Pyle split the other half.

Grange wore Bears colors for the first time against the Chicago Cardinals on November 26, 1925, Thanksgiving Day, at Cubs Park. He gained 92 yards, but the Cardinals star, Paddy Driscoll, punted away from the redhead all day. The game ended in a scoreless tie before 36,000 fans, the largest crowd in pro football history to date. The best was yet to come.

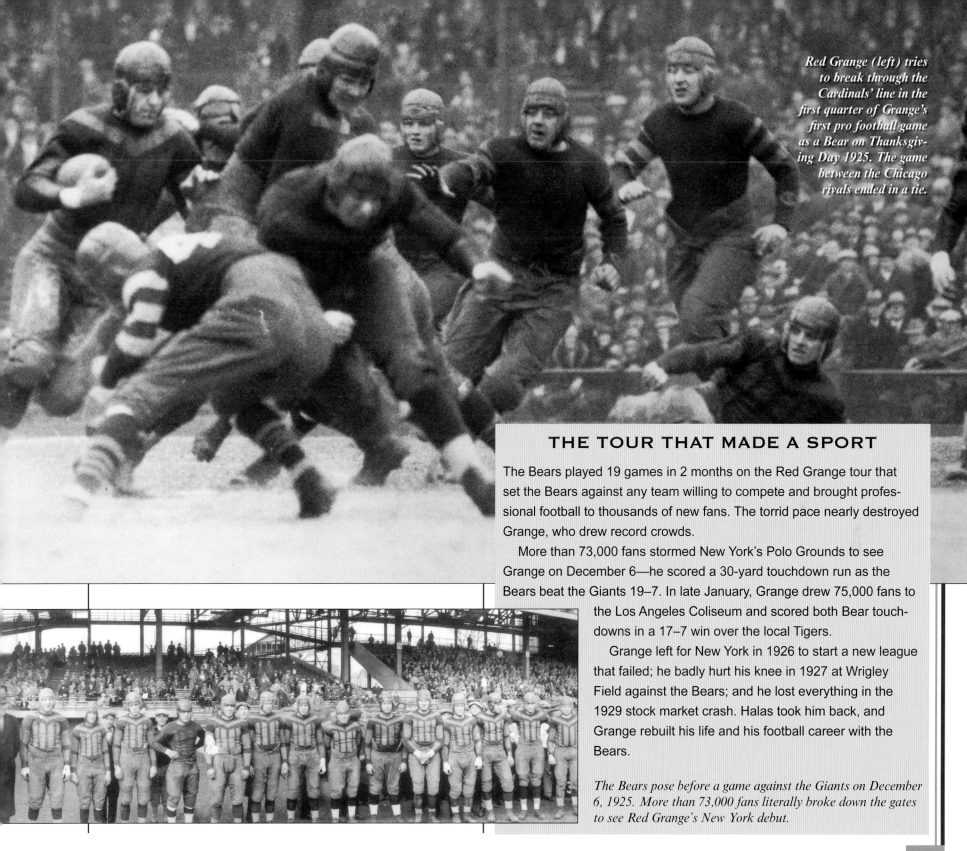

Red Grange (left) tries to break through the Cardinals' line in the first quarter of Grange's first pro football game as a Bear on Thanksgiving Day 1925. The game between the Chicago rivals ended in a tie.

THE TOUR THAT MADE A SPORT

The Bears played 19 games in 2 months on the Red Grange tour that set the Bears against any team willing to compete and brought professional football to thousands of new fans. The torrid pace nearly destroyed Grange, who drew record crowds.

More than 73,000 fans stormed New York's Polo Grounds to see Grange on December 6—he scored a 30-yard touchdown run as the Bears beat the Giants 19–7. In late January, Grange drew 75,000 fans to the Los Angeles Coliseum and scored both Bear touchdowns in a 17–7 win over the local Tigers.

Grange left for New York in 1926 to start a new league that failed; he badly hurt his knee in 1927 at Wrigley Field against the Bears; and he lost everything in the 1929 stock market crash. Halas took him back, and Grange rebuilt his life and his football career with the Bears.

The Bears pose before a game against the Giants on December 6, 1925. More than 73,000 fans literally broke down the gates to see Red Grange's New York debut.

THE T FORMATION COMES TO TOWN

By 1929, a simmering feud between George Halas and Ed Sternaman erupted, and countermanding coaching orders from both men confused the players. After starting at 4–1–1, the team collapsed after the October 24 crash of the stock market. Halas lost his stock portfolio, and his real estate development business was ruined. Sternaman could not raise the cash to handle his apartment buildings and gas stations. On the field, the team managed a single tie in the midst of a nine-game winless streak to finish the season 4–9–2.

The two men were able to reach one last agreement: They hired Lake Forest Academy head coach and athletic director Ralph Jones as the new leader of the Bears. When Halas and Sternaman interviewed Jones in 1930, he promised to bring a championship within three years. Hiring Jones changed the franchise and revolutionized and modernized football.

Sid Luckman demonstrates the fine points of the T formation and the quarterback stance at the line of scrimmage in spring practice at his alma mater, Columbia University. Coach Lou Little (at right) watches his former star with approval.

THE MAN IN MOTION

Putting a back in motion on offense was the revolutionary touch that triggered Ralph Jones's quick-hitting T-formation attack. His key player was the still-dangerous Red Grange, who would take off from his left halfback position before the snap and run laterally across the formation to see what the enemy would do. If the defense did not react by sending a man out to cover him, Grange—the motion man—could then take a pitchout for a sweep or catch a pass either from the quarterback or a fullback such as Bronko Nagurski, who was also an excellent passer. If the opponent did deploy a man to follow Grange, then that left one less defender near the line of scrimmage to stop the Bears' powerful running game. The motion back could further confuse the defense by faking one way before turning to go in the other direction. It was a significant change in the game, pitting brains against brawn.

THE "T" FORMATION

CHICAGO

BY
SID LUCKMAN

In this booklet, Sid Luckman details the secrets of the T formation.

Jones told Halas and Sternaman that he would win with a retooled version of the T formation taught by Bob Zuppke at Illinois. In his version, Jones spaced the linemen and backs to give them operating room. For linemen, finesse became as vital as strength, and for the first time, the Jones system let the center keep his head up and be an effective blocker. The three backs—left half, fullback, and right half—lined up three yards behind the line. The quarterback, as the top of the "T," pivoted to make a handoff or pitchout to a running back or fade back and throw a forward pass. This opened the game to long runs and passes and the potential to score on any play.

JUST HALAS AND THE BEARS

A huge storm in mid-December 1932, covered Wrigley Field with a foot of snow. The conditions forced George Halas to move the title game with the Portsmouth Spartans indoors to the Chicago Stadium.

In the summer of 1931, when George Halas learned that Ed Sternaman was broke, Halas exercised their partnership right to buy him out. After intense negotiations, they agreed on a franchise value of $76,000. Thus, Papa Bear had to find $38,000 to pay for Sternaman's 50 percent share. Halas agreed to put down $25,000 and deliver the rest in two payments over the next calendar year. Halas, who had no money either, found early help from five sources. Ralph Brizzolara, his best friend since high school, came through with $5,000, as did Jim McMillen, a retired Bears lineman who was striking it rich as a professional wrestler. Halas's mother, Barbara, invested another $5,000. The breakthrough, though, came when George Trafton's mother invested $20,000. Halas landed

another $5,000 from his wealthy friend Charles Bidwill. Bidwill owned two racetracks in the Chicago area, Sportsman's Park (now known as the Chicago Motor Speedway) and Hawthorne Race Course, as well as a company that printed most of the tickets for major events in Chicago. For the favor, Halas made Bidwill the team secretary and steered him to the South Side where, in 1933, Bidwill picked up the Cardinals for $50,000. However, he retained his Bears stock until his death in 1947.

The $40,000 cash infusion allowed Halas to pay the $25,000 down payment and make good on several overdue bills. He also still had enough to make his first payment of $6,000 to Sternaman on January 25, 1932. Unfortunately, Halas was now in need of $5,000 for the second installment, and Papa Bear was shocked when he read the fine print in the sale agreement: If he failed to make the final payment by noon on July 31, 1932, he would lose everything to Sternaman—the team and the money!

By July, with most of the banks in America out of business, Halas talked Sternaman into a ten-day extension. He then had until August 9 to come up with the final $5,000. That morning, banker C. K. Anderson from Antioch (on the Illinois-Wisconsin border) called Halas at his Loop office and told him he could get him a check; Halas could pick it up at an office Anderson maintained at Randolph and LaSalle in downtown Chicago. Halas ended up making the final payment with ten minutes to spare. That season, a cash-strapped Halas was forced to issue IOUs to several players, including Grange and Nagurski, but he redeemed every IOU within two years.

Because he had no cash to repay the loans from his friends and family, Papa Bear converted the loans into stock. Each $5,000 was worth $1/12$ of the franchise—8.33 percent. Over the years, he bought out everyone except Brizzolara, whose family cashed in handsomely when they sold the shares in 1987.

BEST OF THE BEARS

Box seats were only $2.20 at Wrigley Field when the Bears played the New York Yankees in 1927. The Bears won 12-0.

Red Grange is the face of the Bears on this program from December 1925—the Grange exhibition tour began after this game. The Giants won 9-0.

Official Program 1925

"77" "77"

Chicago Bears vs. New York Giants
SUNDAY, DEC. 13th 2:15 P. M.

CUBS PARK

Price **10** Cents

JOSEPH P. KENNEDY PRESENTS

THE NATION'S IDOL!

Red Grange

BY ARRANGEMENT WITH C.C. PYLE AND W.E. SHALLENBERGER

IN

ONE MINUTE TO PLAY

A SAM WOOD PRODUCTION

STORY BY BYRON MORGAN

Distributed by GREATER **FBO** FILM BOOKING OFFICES OF AMERICA, INC.

Red Grange starred in the silent-era potboiler One Minute to Play in the summer of 1926. The producer was Joseph P. Kennedy, who battled endlessly with Grange's manager, C. C. Pyle, over money.

Anyone could enjoy the Galloping Ghost's favorite candy bar for just a nickel. Grange cleaned up on endorsements and movie deals until the 1929 stock market crash.

Shotwell's **Red Grange** 5¢

MILK CHOCOLATE NUT BAR

This program marks the first NFL championship game. The Bears beat the Giants 23–21 in a thriller that was decided by Red Grange's game-saving tackle on the final play.

CHICAGO BEARS
FOOTBALL CLUB INC.
WRIGLEY FIELD

OFFICIAL PROGRAM

PRICE 10¢

World's Championship
Sunday, Dec. 17, 1933
•
CHICAGO BEARS
Champions Western Division
vs.
NEW YORK GIANTS
Champions Eastern Division

The 1938 press guide featured Bears players including Joe Stydahar (13); Dick Plasman (14), the last man to play helmetless in the NFL; Jack Manders (10); and holder Gene Ronzani (6).

CHICAGO BEARS
1938 SEASON

Red Grange connects with a young fan in 1934. At that time, every Chicago-area boy emulated Grange in backlot or prairie pick-up games.

On July 20, 1926, the *Chicago Tribune* reveals a growing rift between partners George Halas and Ed Sternaman. Halas won control of the franchise in 1932 when he bought out Sternaman.

THE CHAMPS WHO CAME IN FROM THE COLD

By 1932, the National Football League was down to eight franchises located in only five cities: the Bears and Cardinals in Chicago; the Giants, Brooklyn Dodgers, and Staten Island Stapletons in New York; the Boston Braves; the Portsmouth, Ohio, Spartans; and the Green Bay Packers, who were the winners of three straight titles from 1929 to 1931.

The 1932 league was beset with ties, an unbalanced schedule, and archaic rules. On the morning of December 11, the Bears were 5–1–6 to Portsmouth's 6–1–4. The Bears had to beat Green Bay at Wrigley Field in order to force a playoff with Portsmouth. A raging blizzard that morning held Wrigley Field attendance to 5,000 as Nagurski scored the only touchdown in a 9–0 win over the Packers to earn the playoff.

The bitter arctic cold left Wrigley Field frozen solid under ice. The league, at Halas's urging, moved the playoff game indoors to the Chicago Stadium, where a circus had just finished its run. It was a makeshift affair: After a hurried cleanup to rid the stadium floor of animal droppings, the playing field was short and narrow—only 80 yards long. Both teams agreed to two ground rules: They would use one goalpost that was located on the goal line, and the ball would start in the middle of the field, not where play ended. A noisy crowd of more than 11,000 shook the barn on West Madison Street as both teams struggled to score.

Late in the game, after the Spartans stopped Nagurski three times at the goal line, the Bears ad-libbed a winning play that changed pro football. Nagurski took a direct snap, started for the goal line, then stood up and threw a jump pass into the end zone. Grange, who was on the ground, looked up and made the touchdown catch. Portsmouth complained, in vain, to the officials that Nagurski threw his pass inside the no-passing zone within five yards of the line of scrimmage.

Chicago added a safety to win the first championship played indoors 9–0.

Ralph Jones had fulfilled his promise to win a championship by his third season. With that, Halas announced that he would return to the sidelines in 1933. Jones ended up at Lake Forest College.

In the off-season, Halas and Redskins owner George Preston Marshall rammed through rule changes that allowed passing from anywhere behind the line of scrimmage, created hashmarks ten yards from the sideline to open the field, and placed the goalposts on the goal line. One final, major rule change divided the league into Eastern and Western divisions, with a season-ending championship game between the winners of each division.

The Bears won their second title by beating the Portsmouth Spartans on the floor of the Chicago Stadium on December 18, 1932. The stadium was littered with animal droppings from the just-departed circus. Note the single goalpost and that most men wore hats.

STARS OF THE 1930s

George Halas always called the 6′2″, 230-pound **Bronko Nagurski** the greatest football player he ever coached. He was so good at the University of Minnesota that *The New York Sun*'s 1929 All-America team featured just ten offensive players—Nagurski filled both the fullback and tackle positions.

During one practice in early 1930, the equally legendary Red Grange tried to bring down the big man. "When you hit Bronk at the ankles," Grange said, "it was like an electric shock. If you hit him above the ankles, you were likely to get killed."

Nagurski retired after the 1937 season at the relatively early age of 29. Halas was willing to pay him only $5,000, but Nagurski could earn more than that as a professional wrestler.

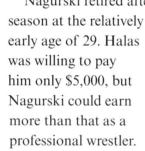

Bronko Nagurski

The decision turned out to be a wise one regardless of the money involved; he went on to be World Heavyweight Champion several times over.

One of the reasons Nagurski was so great in 1934 was the play of his running mate in the Bears' backfield, rookie halfback **Beattie Feathers.** Feathers set two league rushing records that season when he gained 1,004 yards on the ground and averaged 8.4 yards per carry. He left the team for Brooklyn after the 1937 season, although he never enjoyed near the success with the Dodgers that he did with Nagurski and the Bears.

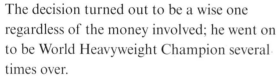

Beattie Feathers

End **Bill Hewitt,** who starred in Chicago from 1932 to 1936, was another of Halas's all-time favorites. Quick on the pass rush as a defender and equally clever on the offensive side of the ball, Hewitt was one of the last NFL players who refused to wear a helmet. In 1949, two years after Hewitt's untimely death in an auto crash, the Bears became the first team to retire uniform numbers. In addition to Grange's number 77 and Nagurski's number 3, Hewitt's number 56 was one of the original honorees.

Danny Fortmann

George Musso accepted Halas's $90 per-game offer, as well as a $5 check to cover his train fare from Millikin University in Decatur to Chicago in 1932. Musso had the distinction of playing against two future presidents. Nicknamed "Moose," he squared off against Ronald Reagan in 1929, when Millikin played Eureka College, and he also opposed Gerald Ford of Michigan, when the Bears faced the College All-Stars in 1934. Musso was an All-Pro at tackle and guard as well as a team captain for eight seasons.

In 1936, at age 20, **Danny Fortmann** was a guard, a Phi Beta Kappa, and a pre-med student from Colgate when he began the first of eight All-Pro seasons. Halas paid his tuition to the University of Chicago Medical School, where Fortmann eventually became Dr. Fortmann after earning his degree in medicine in 1940.

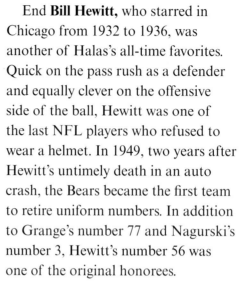

1933: HALAS RETAKES THE HELM

Before the 1933 season, George Halas cut a deal with Hunk Anderson, his friend and the coach at Notre Dame: Pro football's first training camp would be held on the South Bend campus. The Bears also became the first to film each play in order to help the coaches produce battle plans.

The defending-champion Bears closed the regular season with four straight wins to clinch the Western Division title with a 10–2–1 record. Their opponents in the first NFL title game on December 17, before 26,000 fans at Wrigley Field, were the Eastern champions, the New York Giants.

In a back-and-forth struggle that produced six lead changes, this was a championship game worthy of that moniker. The Bears came out in white jerseys with blue trim, orange pants, and 20 orange helmets for 22 players—tough guys Bill Hewitt and George Musso scorned headgear.

The Giants held a 21–16 fourth-quarter lead when the Bears started a late drive. With the ball at the New York 33-yard line and just a minute left, Bears quarterback Carl Brumbaugh called a play dreamed up by Hewitt earlier: a pass and lateral to a trailer that they called the "Stinky Special." Bronko Nagurski took a direct snap and fired down the right side to Hewitt at the 19-yard line. Hewitt turned and—just as Hewitt had envisioned it in his mind—sent a lateral to Bill Karr, who scored on the miracle play to give the Bears a 23–21 lead.

The Giants had time for one more play. Harry Newman threw downfield to Dale Burnett, who was wide open. In an instant, defender Red Grange saw the Giants center, Mel Hein, trailing Burnett. Grange wrapped his arms around the Giants receiver and pinned his arms to his body to prevent a lateral, bringing Burnett down before he could flip the ball to Hein at the final gun. Halas called it the greatest defensive play he ever saw. The Bears were the first champions of the modern National Football League.

THE SNEAKERS GAME

The Bears won all 13 regular season games in 1934, extending their winning streak to 18. They were heavily favored to win the title on December 9 against the Giants. A bitter nor'easter drowned New York on December 8, and overnight temperatures plunged to nine degrees above zero. On game day, the field was a lumpy skating rink, with players sliding all over the place.

Inspired by one of his player's comments about needing sneakers to beat the ice, Giants trainer Gus Mauch dispatched clubhouse attendant Abe Cohen to Manhattan College to pick up basketball shoes. The Bears had a 13–3 lead in the fourth quarter when Cohen arrived with the sneakers.

The Giants now had traction and the edge. New York ran off 27 unanswered points to win the title 30–13. George Halas always called that disaster the "rubber shoes game." Chicago's championship run was over.

Bronko Nagurski plows for several yards as the Bears open an early 13–3 lead in the 1934 title game with New York at the Polo Grounds on December 9. Wearing sneakers to gain sure footing, the Giants scored 27 fourth-quarter points to beat the Bears 30–13.

GAME DAY: 1930s

By 1939, the Bears, the team with the most wins in the National Football League, were seeking the same public acceptance that baseball enjoyed. George Halas was charging $2.20 for a box seat and just a dollar for the bleachers. He increased capacity by using his own narrow-seated folding chairs so he could then shoehorn ten chairs into a box—baseball seated just eight people in the same space.

With the exception of visits from rival Green Bay, the Bears played to many empty seats. On November 7, 1937, fans watched the Packers beat the Bears by the score of 24–14. That was the only Bears defeat until the championship game against the Redskins on December 12, when miserable cold held down the crowd to around 15,000. Rookie Sammy Baugh crushed the Bears with three long scoring passes in the third quarter. In its first season in Washington, the transplanted Boston franchise gained a 28–21 victory, as well as the championship.

The Bears' uniform also evolved over the years. By the '30s, game-day uniforms were white jerseys with three black stripes around the biceps and either orange or blue pants, or they donned orange jerseys with black piping and numbers. In 1939, after trying several helmet combinations, George Halas outfitted the team in the solid black/navy blue helmet they wear to this day.

Since the league's founding in 1920, Bears fans had watched their team win three championships and two division titles and don new helmets. Additionally, a brilliant 1939 draft led by top-pick quarterback Sid Luckman, second first-round pick, fullback Bill Osmanski, and seventh-round guard Ray Bray allowed many fans to witness the pieces falling in place for the dynasty that would eventually become the Monsters of the Midway.

On December 8, 1935, Red Grange tracks down the Cardinals runner at Wrigley Field as the Bears roll over the Big Red 13–0. Note the many empty seats on this cold day in the depth of the Depression.

CHAPTER TWO

MONSTERS OF THE MIDWAY

1940–1963

"The weather was perfect. So were the Bears. In the most fearsome display of power ever seen on any gridiron, the Monsters of the Midway won the Ed Thorp Trophy, symbolic of the league championship."

ARTHUR DALEY, *THE NEW YORK TIMES*, DECEMBER 9, 1940

Above: *This pennant honors the 1946 champion Chicago Bears.* **Right:** *John Siegal (6) burst into the New York Giants secondary in the 1941 championship game at Wrigley Field with teammates Bill Osmanski (9), George McAfee (5), Ray Bray (82, on the ground), Lee Artoe (35), and Ed Kolman (29). The Bears won the game 37–9.*

73–0

The Bears served notice at Green Bay in the September 22, 1940, opener when they routed the defending champion Packers 41–0. But the critical mass boiled over in Washington on November 17, when the Redskins escaped with a 7–3 win. The Bears growled after the defeat—they felt they were cheated out of a winning touchdown on a noninterference call in the end zone. When Redskins owner George Preston Marshall called them crybabies in the newspapers, Halas quickly took charge. He handled the psychology himself and then called in Clark Shaughnessy, who had just finished an acclaimed 9–0 season at Stanford. Shaughnessy, using the updated T formation he and Halas had devised, installed a game plan for what would be a historic December 8 rematch.

On film, Shaughnessy saw that Redskins defenders did not adjust to the man in motion. So he sprung a trap: He told Luckman to start with a handoff to McAfee from his right halfback position on a quick opener, with Ray Nolting going in motion before the snap to his right.

Above: *The Griffith Stadium scoreboard on December 8, 1940, in Washington, D.C., shows a 60–0 Bears lead. The referee asked George Halas to stop kicking for extra points and have his team run instead—they'd kicked the other balls into the crowd. The Bears won the championship 73–0.* **Left:** *Sid Luckman is featured on the 1941 championship game program cover. The Bears beat the New York Giants 37–9 for the Bears fifth title.*

The play gained seven yards. More importantly, Luckman saw that Washington did not follow Nolting.

A fullback counter followed. Lining up at his right halfback position once again, McAfee ran in motion across the formation. At the snap, Nolting and fullback Osmanski both faked right then cut left—this looked to be their usual counterplay. Washington took the bait, and Luckman handed off to Osmanski, who swung toward the sideline and then cut up field quickly—true to his nickname, "Bullet Bill."

Near midfield, right end George Wilson erased two Washington defenders with a devastating blindside block, and Osmanski sprinted to a 68-yard touchdown.

The Bears never looked back as they took a 28–0 halftime lead, adding 26 points in the third quarter and 19 more in the fourth for a 73–0 victory. They gained 382 yards on the ground, added 119 in the air on seven of ten pass completions, and returned three of their eight interceptions for touchdowns. Ten men scored the 11 TDs, with backup Harry Clark getting two. When the officials informed both teams that they were running out of footballs—kicked for all those extra points, the balls were kept by fans after they flew into the stands—Halas had the Bears run or pass for the extra points instead. As Arthur Daley wrote in *The New York Times,* "At this moment, the Chicago Bears are the greatest team of all time."

"BEAR DOWN, CHICAGO BEARS"

The Bears 73–0 win over the Redskins for the championship is still the largest shutout margin of any game in NFL history. A year later, in 1941, George Halas introduced a fight song to honor his team. "Bear Down, Chicago Bears" was composed by Al Hoffman (under the pseudonym Jerry Downs), a hit songwriter who also penned "If I Knew You Were Comin', I'd've Baked a Cake" and is a member of the Songwriters Hall of Fame. The song pays tribute to the Bears' 1940 victory and claims them as a source of pride for the state of Illinois. It has been used as the team's anthem since its introduction and is played at home games every time the Bears score.

BEARS VERSUS CARDINALS

The Bears and Packers make up the National Football League's most enduring rivalry, with 177 games played between the two clubs since 1921. That competition, however, doesn't compare to the Chicago Bears versus Chicago Cardinals in terms of nastiness, outright hatred, and enduring passion. Senior residents on the Windy City's South Side still curse George Halas for chasing the Big Red out of town half a century ago.

The Cardinals started playing semipro football in 1898 and were originally knows as the Morgan Athletic Club. Along with Halas and the Decatur Staleys, they were original signers of the American Professional Football Association charter at Canton, Ohio, in 1920. The rivalry turned real in 1921, when Halas moved the Staleys to Cubs Park and subsequently put together the league's elite team. And it was aggravated even further when Halas fiercely pursued Cardinals franchise player Paddy Driscoll before finally landing him for the 1926 season—the same year the Cardinals claimed the NFL title.

In 1933, at Halas's urging, one of his investors, Charles Bidwill, bought the Cardinals for $50,000. Then in 1936, Halas convinced Bidwill to sign the "Madison Street Agreement," which stipulated that each team could only operate on its own side of the street that divided Chicago's North and South sides. In turn, Bidwill retained his Bears stock and was going to sell it back to Halas, but he died unexpectedly in 1947.

The Bears went 45–19–6 against their crosstown rivals in the Cardinals' 40 years in Chicago, but the Cardinals played the spoiler on at least two occasions. Old timers relish the 1951 finale in the bitter cold at Wrigley Field, when the 2-9 Cardinals knocked the heavily favored Bears out of title contention with a 24–14 upset. With just a minute left and the contest all but decided, Charley Trippi, who endured years of punishment from the Bears' notoriously nasty Eddie Sprinkle, walked up to his tormenter and KO'd him with a right cross.

But the Cardinals' supreme moment came in a late 1955 snowstorm at Comiskey Park, when they derailed the Bears' title express in a 53–14 massacre. The Bears did not win a championship in the entire decade of the 1950s, but the disappointment of that '55 squad must have really taken its toll on Halas—Papa Bear turned the head-coaching reins over to Driscoll the following season.

In 1959, the Cardinals moved to Soldier Field, where they played to mostly empty seats. But when club president Walter Wolfner wanted to move to Northwestern's Dyche Stadium in Evanston to draw more fans, Halas dug into his desk and invoked the old Madison Street Agreement—and that was it for the Cardinals in the great city of Chicago. They flew off to St. Louis on March 13, 1960.

Above: *Billy Cross of the Cardinals takes off on a 39-yard touchdown run as the South Siders upset the favored Bears 28–14 at Comiskey Park on October 7, 1951.* **Left:** *This ticket stub is from a Cardinals-Bears game on December 2, 1945, at Comiskey. The Bears won 28–20.*

No. 3240
WEST STAND - $1.80
Est. Price $1.50 — Gov't Tax 30c
CARDINALS VS.
BEARS — DEC. 2
Comiskey Park
No Money Refunded
RETAIN THIS TICKET
32 BENTLEY, MURRAY CO.

MONSTERS OF THE MIDWAY

From 1940 to 1946, the Chicago Bears were the original Monsters of the Midway, and the 73–0 game was their touchstone. George Halas, though, always called the 1941 Bears his masterpiece.

Each of the 33 men on his team had All-Pro credentials. When George McAfee broke a long run, kick return, or interception runback, his replacement, Hugh Gallarneau, was just as dangerous. Ditto for fullbacks Norm Standlee, Gary Famiglietti, or Joe Maniaci when they relieved Bill Osmanski or Bob Swisher and Ray McLean when they backed Ray Nolting. In 11 games, the 1941 Bears scored 396 points—an average of 36 points per game, prorated to 576 over today's 16-game season.

The Bears dealt the Packers their only loss, 25–17, in the opener at Green Bay. The Packers returned the favor mid-season with a 16–14 win at Wrigley Field, which set up the NFL's first divisional playoff, also at Wrigley Field, on December 14—a week after Pearl Harbor. The Bears broke it open with a 24-point second quarter and a

Sid Luckman, the original T formation quarterback, gets ready to uncork a long pass against the New York Giants at the Polo Grounds on November 14, 1943. The Bears won 56–7, aided by Luckman's seven touchdown passes.

THE BEARS AND THE NFL GO TO WAR

Members of the Bears went off to war in 1942, including George McAfee, Joe Maniaci, Bill Hughes, Ken Kavanaugh, Dick Plasman (the NFL's last helmetless player), and Young Bussey. Lieutenant Bussey, backup quarterback to Sid Luckman, died on January 7, 1945, in the Battle of Lingayen Gulf in the Philippines, the only Bear killed in World War II action.

Like his players, Reserve Lieutenant Commander George Halas said farewell to the Wrigley Field fans and the Bears and reported for active duty with the Navy on November 2, 1942. The coach served on the staff of Pacific commander Admiral Chester Nimitz.

Nineteen of the 28 members of the 1943 championship team also left for war, including medical doctor Danny Fortmann, dentist Bill Osmanski, and Merchant Marine Luckman. Stationed stateside, Luckman was given permission to continue to play in Bears games.

267-yard ground attack, led by rookie fullback Standlee; the team overwhelmed Green Bay 33–14 before 43,425 fans. Only 13,000 turned out a week later to see the Bears rout the Giants for their fifth title. Incidentally, McLean iced the 37–9 victory with the last drop-kicked conversion until New England's Doug Flutie converted in 2006.

The 1942 team won all 11 league games to raise the team's winning streak to 18, which set up a 1940 title rematch in Washington. After the Bears took a 6–0 lead on tackle Lee Artoe's 50-yard run with a fumble, the Redskins took charge, scored twice, and shut the Bears down. They avenged the 73–0 thrashing and won the title 14–6.

By 1943, most of the stars, including owner/coach Halas, were off to war. Sid Luckman remained, and the Bears assembled enough talent to deliver the goods. Best of all, co-head coach Hunk Anderson talked Bronko Nagurski out

Above: *Sid Luckman zips through a big hole at Wrigley Field on December 26, 1943, as the Bears beat Washington 41–21 for their third title in four years.* **Above right:** *The Monsters of the Midway, honored on this sign, won four championships in the '40s: 1940, 1941, 1943, and 1946.*

of retirement for one last hurrah, which came in the regular season windup at Comiskey Park on November 28. The Cardinals held a 24–14 lead when Anderson sent Nagurski in as fullback. As the crowd roared, Luckman gave the ball time and again to Nagurski, who smashed, fought, and crawled for every inch to score a touchdown. After that exhibition of strength and grit, Luckman put away the Big Red for a 35–24 Bears win.

A month later, Halas came home on Christmas leave to watch the title game at Wrigley Field, again versus the Redskins. Nagurski scored the last touchdown of his career in the second quarter to give the Bears a 14–7 lead, and Luckman threw five touchdown passes to trigger a 41–21 win for their third championship in four years.

Almost everyone returned from war in 1946, and the Bears battled to reach the title game against the Giants at the Polo Grounds. Two Giants were questioned the night before the matchup regarding a bribe attempt by small-time gambler Alvin Paris, who wanted to fix the game. Merle Hapes was barred from playing; Frank Filchock denied any involvement and played with distinction.

The score was tied 14–14 in the fourth quarter. In a pre-arranged code with Halas, Luckman said "Now?" for a bootleg play they called "Bingo Keep It." Halas replied, "Now!" and Luckman faked a handoff to McAfee on a sweep left, kept it as he swung right, and raced for the score. The Bears went on to win 24–14 for their fourth title of the decade and seventh overall.

By 1949, Johnny Lujack (left) had taken over as starting quarterback for Sid Luckman (right). A great all-around star, Lujack quit the Bears in 1951, after just four seasons.

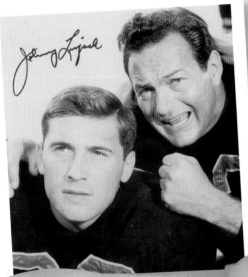

In 1958, a fan could see a Bears game from great seats in the east side temporary bleachers for just $4.50. The Bears won this battle with the Packers 24–10.

The Bears won 58–27 over the Colts, honoring the golden anniversary of the A. E. Staley Mfg. Co. that backed George Halas when he founded the Bears' predecessor in 1920.

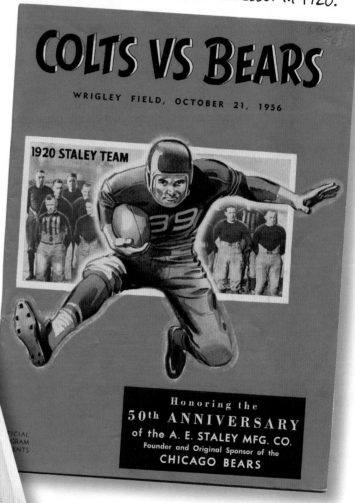

On December 15, 1941, the *Chicago Daily Tribune* Bears' game photo details Hugh Gallarneau's first-quarter, 82-yard touchdown. The Bears won 33–14 at Wrigley Field.

George "One Play" McAfee is shown in action. George Halas said of the Hall of Famer, "Any back compared to McAfee should be honored." He was a premier runner, defender, and punt/kick returner.

BEARS vs. PACKERS

OFFICIAL
15c
PROGRAM

JERRY KEEFE.

Sunday, Nov. 7 — Wrigley Field

This 1943 official program was for the 71st renewal of the NFL's greatest rivalry: the Bears versus the Packers. The Bears won 28-23 with the second of two fourth-quarter touchdowns.

This '40s vintage pennant celebrates the Bears and their home field.

CHICAGO BEARS

This helmet was signed by Hall of Fame linebacker/tackle George Connor. Connor was all-NFL five times.

HUNK AND LUKE

After George Halas coached the Bears to a 45–14 win over the Philadelphia Eagles on October 25, 1942, he made Heartley "Hunk" Anderson and Luke Johnsos co-head coaches. Both men played with Papa Bear in the '20s and became assistants afterward.

Anderson arrived in 1922 from Notre Dame as a 165-pound guard. Until 1927, he played for the Bears on Sundays and served his mentor and friend, Knute Rockne, as line coach on weekdays after his day job as a plant engineer in South Bend. When Rockne was killed in a 1931 plane crash, Anderson became the Notre Dame head coach until 1933. He rejoined Halas in 1940 as a line coach and defensive coordinator.

Johnsos, an end, joined the Bears in 1929 from the Northwestern campus. He played on the other side of the line from Bill Hewitt, became a player/coach in 1935, and served as an assistant in 1937. From 1940 to the end of his coaching career in 1968, Johnsos's game-day station was the press box, where he sent down play suggestions by messenger. One day in 1940,

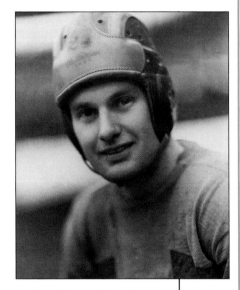

Luke Johnsos, shown here in 1930, was an end for the Bears before becoming their head coach (with Hunk Anderson) in the 1940s. He was first-team All-Pro twice.

when he complained about the slowness of the messenger system, Halas said, "Why not use a telephone?" So Johnsos devised the "eye in the sky" phone system that every team at every level uses to call plays and formations and make suggestions.

When Halas departed for active duty in the Navy, the Anderson/Johnsos combination took charge. Hunk ran the defense, Luke the offense. In their first year and a half, the Bears went 15–2–1, which included the 1943 title after Anderson convinced Bronko Nagurski to come out of retirement. With virtually no players left by 1944, Anderson and Johnsos pulled a miracle with a 6–3–1 season. Their run ended in 1945, when the Bears, who were 1–7, rallied with victories over the Pittsburgh Steelers and the Cardinals, with the help of the returning George McAfee, Ken Kavanaugh, and Joe Stydahar, to finish 3–7. By then, Halas was back home and ready to resume control in 1946, his roster chock full of returning service veterans he hoped could still play.

Hunk Anderson and Luke Johnsos enjoyed a legacy as the 1943 championship coaches. Commander Halas came home on Christmas leave to watch that title game. An hour before the kickoff, Anderson walked to the front of the dressing room and ordered out all visitors. "That means you, too, George," Hunk said to his uniformed boss. Halas laughed as he departed for his seat near the bench, happy to comply.

Halas (far left) gives instructions to his coaching staff, (left to right) Paddy Driscoll, Anderson, and Johnsos, before the 1942 season.

THE PRIDE OF SID LUCKMAN

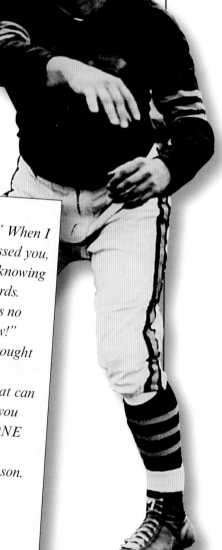

The quarterback of George Halas's and Clark Shaughnessy's dreams had to be the brains and the heart of the offense. Halas found that quarterback in 1938 at Columbia University's Baker Field, when he scouted single-wing tailback Sid Luckman (shown at left on the cover of *LIFE* the same year), a marvelous scholar and athlete from Brooklyn. Luckman had everything Halas sought: the arm, speed, footwork, play-fake ability, intelligence, and leadership.

Before the 1939 draft, George Halas traded Edgar "Eggs" Manske to Pittsburgh for the rights to the second-overall draft selection, which turned out to be Sid Luckman. Halas convinced him to sign—Luckman initially wasn't interested in a career in professional football—for $5,000, the most he'd paid any player since Bronko Nagurski in 1930. Halas later said there were only two people he considered worthy of that salary: Luckman and Jesus Christ.

It was football love at first sight—for both men. And Luckman's teammates felt the same, as he fueled the dynasty that won four NFL titles in seven years. Luckman retired after the 1950 season and was elected to the Pro Football Hall of Fame in 1965. Luckman died in 1998, but had become a rich man in business and earned a well-deserved reputation for generosity long after his playing days. Most of all, he retained the lifelong admiration of his mentor, George Halas, who wrote a remarkable letter dated May 24, 1983, five months before Halas's death.

SID'S DREAM DAY

Sid Luckman's statistics on November 14, 1943, at New York's Polo Grounds still jump off the page more than 65 years later: 23 completions in 30 passes, 433 yards, 7 touchdowns. Bears 56, Giants 7.

Luckman's first football visit to New York since his rookie year in 1939 was billed as "Sid Luckman Day." Admirers from Brooklyn presented him with a $1,000 war bond, and his teammates matched it with a $1,000 bond of their own. As William D. Richardson wrote the next day in *The New York Times,* "Right there was when the Giants and Giant fans made their mistake by not matching or out-donating the other donors. Sid seemed to take it as a personal affront."

My Dear Sid,

"I love you with all my heart." When I said this to you last night as I kissed you, I realized 44 wonderful years of knowing you were summed up by seven words.

My boy, my pride in you knows no bounds. Remember our word "now!" Every time I said it to you, you brought me another championship.

You added a luster to my life that can never tarnish. My devoted friend, you have a spot in my heart that NO ONE else can claim.

God bless you and keep you, my son. "I love you with all my heart."

Sincerely, yours,

George

TV'S ORIGINAL SPORTS IMPRESARIO

In 1947, the city of Chicago had one television station, WBKB, and just 7,000 sets. By 1951, when the first transcontinental telecast linked the coasts, Chicago had four stations and America had millions of sets.

Early in 1947, George Halas's friend, city editor Don Maxwell, invited him to the *Chicago Tribune* for a television demonstration. As they watched the blurry black and white pictures, Maxwell told Halas to imagine seeing his Bears on television; he also said that *Tribune* publisher Colonel Robert R. McCormick was going to start his own station, WGN-TV, in 1948. But Halas really took notice when Maxwell said he could reach an audience many times larger than Wrigley Field's 50,000-person seating capacity.

A few days later, Halas called on Captain Bill Eddy, the general manager at WBKB, hoping to buy time on the station. He was delighted when he walked away with a $5,400 check—$900 per game—for agreeing to air the Bears home games. A year later, after he sold 51,000 tickets to the 1948 season-ender with the Cardinals, Halas let both WBKB, using Red Grange, and WGN-TV, with Jack Brickhouse at the mic, televise the game. That double telecast netted Halas far more than Eddy had paid a year earlier.

Things fell apart in 1949, when Halas let WGN-TV televise the finale with the Cardinals. A heavy rain held the crowd in the stadium to under 15,000 as most of the no-shows watched the game on TV in bars or at home. It was the last Bears telecast for two years.

Fearful that home TV would kill the live gate, Halas convinced NFL Commissioner Bert Bell to institute a league policy in 1951 that would black out local telecasts within a 75-mile radius of the home team's field. That policy held forth until Congress nixed it in 1974. Also in 1951, Halas invited the Cardinals to join him in televising home games to a network of out-of-town stations. Bears business manager Rudy Custer

Shown here are George Halas (left) and Bert Bell (right). Bell was Halas's close friend and the commissioner Halas put in place in 1945. Halas convinced Bell to put Sunday league games on network television in 1956. Bell came back with a CBS regular-season deal and an NBC contract for championship games.

ran the network, and by 1954, while using ABC facilities, it was considered the largest network for independent television. It stretched from Minneapolis to Indianapolis, from Louisville to Miami and New Orleans, and then west to Dallas, Phoenix, and Los Angeles.

Then, in 1956, Commissioner Bell got CBS to pay the league $1 million for the Sunday schedule. A half century later, CBS, NBC, FOX, and ESPN paid the league more than $3.7 billion a year to televise their games. Thanks to Halas, every owner became rich beyond imagination before the first ticket was sold.

BEST RECORD, NO TITLES

From 1947 to 1951, the Bears won 43 regular season games and had 17 losses. It was the best five-year record in the National Football League, but they ended with nothing to show for it. Ironically, in two of those seasons, 1947 and 1948, they weren't even the best team in Chicago.

In 1948, Halas rebuilt the team around two great Notre Dame rookies. The 1947 Heisman Trophy winner, quarterback Johnny Lujack, came to camp and beat out Sid Luckman for the starting quarterback position. Lujack was an all-league defensive back and handled the punting and place kicking. His Fighting Irish teammate, George Connor, became a perennial All-Pro and Hall of Fame tackle and linebacker.

The crosstown Cardinals, in the only taste of success in their long history, beat the Bears in the 1947 and 1948 season finales to capture the Western Division both times. While the Bears sat at home in 1947, the Cardinals went on to beat the Philadelphia Eagles 28–21 at Comiskey Park on December 28, 1947, for the league title. In 1948, the Bears and the Cardinals, both at 10–1, entered the December 12 finale at Wrigley Field. The Bears were leading 21–10 in the fourth quarter, but the Cardinals pulled out all the stops and scored two late touchdowns to win the Western title 24–21. The following week, in the blinding snow and bitter cold of Philly's Shibe Park, the Eagles shut them out 7–0.

The Bears went 9–3 in 1949, but they lost two games to the Los Angeles Rams, who were coached by Clark Shaughnessy, and fell short of a Western title. The next year, in 1950, they went 9–3 to tie the Rams for the Western title. In a playoff on December 17, the Rams beat the Bears 24–14.

The 1951 Bears also came up short; they lost four of their last six games and finished fourth behind the eventual league champions, the Los Angeles Rams, the second-place Detroit Lions, and the third-place San Francisco 49ers. The Monsters of the Midway dynasty was history.

LUJACK'S GREATEST DAY AS A BEAR

Everything had to click on December 11, 1949, for the Bears to reach the NFL championship game. They had to beat the Cardinals at Wrigley Field, while the Washington Redskins had to beat the Los Angeles Rams later that afternoon.

The city of Chicago woke up that morning to a downpour that never eased; only 15,000 fans showed up—most people watched the game on television. But everything worked for second-year quarterback Johnny Lujack. When it was over, Lujack was 24 for 40 for a league-record 468 yards. Two Bear receivers, end Ken Kavanaugh and fullback John Hoffman, each caught two of Lujack's six scoring passes. Unfortunately for the Bears, the Rams pounded the Redskins 53–27, nullifying Lujack's record-setting day.

George Halas, assistant Hunk Anderson, and Sid Luckman (42) congratulate rookie quarterback Johnny Lujack (32) on his NFL-record game on December 11, which the Bears won 52–21. Some of the other Bears in row two include Bulldog Turner (66), Ray Bray (82), and Chuck Drulis (21).

CHANGING TIMES

hen the time came to integrate his roster, George Halas was one of many owners to take action. Before 1960, African Americans were chosen for speed and used as running backs, defensive backs, and receivers. They were also chosen in even numbers so teams could pair them off as roommates on road trips.

Halas started with College of Pacific halfback Eddie Macon, chosen in the second round of the 1952 draft. A year later, Halas used his first pick on sprinter/receiver Billy Anderson. By 1954, however, both men washed out after minimal contributions.

But the NFL's first black quarterback, 5′11″ Willie Thrower—a free agent despite winning a national championship at Michigan State—made history even though he only suited up in one career game. On October 13, 1953, in relief of starter George Blanda, Thrower completed three of eight passes for 27 yards. His last NFL play was an interception in that 35–28 loss to the San Francisco 49ers. The Bears cut him the next year. It would be another 15 years before a black quarterback would line up under center in the NFL.

The next set of African American players for the Bears included Bobby Watkins and J. C. Caroline. Watkins was a

George Halas and the Bears are jubilant after beating the 49ers 28–6 in the 1958 home opener at Wrigley Field. Four black players had joined the roster: Bobby Watkins (45) and Erich Barnes (24) in the middle row and Willie Galimore (28) and J. C. Caroline (25) in front.

J. C. Caroline, out of Illinois, was the 1956 NFL Rookie of the Year and an all-time Halas favorite. Nearly blind in one eye, he was a superb corner-back and sure tackler who played ten outstanding seasons. In his later years, he was the best special teams player in the NFL.

1955 second-round pick from Ohio State who eventually became a starting halfback and played through '58. Caroline, an Illinois defensive back, was a Pro Bowler and NFL Rookie of the Year in 1956. Caroline's sure tackling on special teams kept him in the league through '65. The exciting Willie Galimore also burst into stardom in 1958 and played through the '63 championship season, when he broke open the Packers rematch with a 27-yard touchdown run.

Finally, Halas landed a championship defensive back in 1961 with Rosey Taylor. Taylor starred at free safety, leading the league with nine interceptions in '63. He was traded to San Francisco midway through the 1969 season and finished his career with Washington in '72.

George Halas called Willie Galimore the best open field back in the league. Galimore recovered from double knee surgery to excel in the 1963 championship season but was killed in 1964 with John Farrington in an auto crash at Rensselaer training camp.

GEORGE TALIAFERRO, THE ONE WHO GOT AWAY

In Round 13 of the 1949 draft, the Bears became the first NFL team to draft a black player. George Taliaferro, a lifelong Bears fan from Gary, Indiana, was a star tailback of Indiana's 1945 Big Ten championship team, but he had already signed with the AAFC Los Angeles Dons. When Taliaferro's father reminded him that he took the Dons' bonus check, Taliaferro told Halas he had to honor his previous commitment.

Taliaferro became AAFC Rookie of the Year in 1949 and then joined the New York Yanks in the 1950 merger. He finished his career in 1955 with the Eagles. When Halas asked Taliaferro to join the Bears for the 1956 season, Taliaferro said he could not take money under false pretenses; he retired to enter higher education.

In 1949, the Bears made Indiana back George Taliaferro the first African American chosen in the NFL draft. Unfortunately, he had already signed with Los Angeles in the AAFC. Taliaferro joined the NFL in 1950 but never played for the Bears.

1950: A BAKER'S DOZEN

*C*hicago Tribune sports editor Arch Ward founded the All-America Football Conference (AAFC) in 1944 because of a dispute with George Halas—it was a big money battle Ward could not win. Ward was furious that Halas refused to grant a Los Angeles NFL franchise to his friends Chicago horse-racing mogul Ben Lindheimer and his partner, actor Don Ameche. No one knew that Halas had already promised Los Angeles to Cardinals owner Charlie Bidwill. In return for the franchise, Bidwill was to give his Bears stock to Halas and forgive Papa Bear's debt from the 1932 buyout of former partner Ed Sternaman. When Halas returned home

George Halas's friendship with Chicago Tribune sports editor Arch Ward ended in 1944 due to Halas's refusal to grant a Los Angeles NFL franchise to Ward's friends. Ward's All-America Football Conference waged a costly war with the NFL through 1949.

in 1945, however, he encouraged Bidwill to keep his team in Chicago, thus enabling Cleveland Rams owner Dan Reeves (who had just beat Washington for the NFL title) to move to Los Angeles instead. Having a winning NFL team there was what Halas preferred, but it only fueled the feud.

The best teams of Ward's AAFC were the 49ers, a Lindheimer/Ameche partnership he set up to operate as the Los Angeles Dons, and the superb team organized by Ohio State's 1942 national champion coach Paul Brown—the Cleveland Browns. While serving as coach at Great Lakes Naval Training Center, Lieutenant Brown signed the elite service players, the most prominent being Northwestern's Otto Graham. Upgrading the George Halas/Clark Shaughnessy T formation, Brown built an offense around Graham as the quarterback. He also constructed a superior defense. The Browns thoroughly dominated the AAFC, winning all four championships.

When the owners called a ceasefire to what had escalated into the 1946–1949 Pro Football War, only the Bears and Washington Redskins were making money in the National Football League. The Cleveland Browns and San Francisco 49ers were the only teams operating in the black in the All-America Football Conference.

In the 1950 merger with the AAFC, NFL strongmen Halas and George Preston Marshall (of the Washington Redskins) accepted three new teams—Cleveland, San Francisco, and Baltimore—creating a 13-team league. Halas put the Browns in the east, now called the American Conference, and kicked the Cardinals out of the west, now called the National Conference. He installed the 49ers in the American Conference and placed the New York Yanks in the National Conference. The dominos fell: Baltimore's Colts failed after one season; New York moved to Dallas in 1952 and also failed. But Baltimore got a second chance for the Colts in 1953 and succeeded.

The Bears opened the 1950 season with back-to-back West Coast games. They beat the Rams 24–20 and the 49ers 32–20; however, they lost the National Division playoff to the Rams 24–14. The following week, the Browns gave the late AAFC bragging rights as they beat the Rams 30–28 for the NFL title.

PADDY DRISCOLL:
THE "YOUNGER" MAN

In early 1955, George Halas announced that to honor his wife, Min, he would retire as coach at season's end. Speculation on his successor centered on assistant Luke Johnsos, co-coach of the 1943 champions—the natural choice.

Defying all logic, though, Papa Bear announced on February 2, 1956, his 61st birthday, that he was turning over his team to a "younger man," his old friend Paddy Driscoll—who was actually born 22 days *before* Halas. The move allowed Halas to devote his time and energy to saving the troubled Green Bay franchise. He led a successful bond issue drive to replace the team's 22,000-seat wooden relic of a stadium with the modern one that became Lambeau Field.

John "Paddy" Driscoll was an All-America triple-threat tailback at Northwestern, in his hometown of Evanston, Illinois, before he met Ensign Halas on the Great Lakes football team in 1918. Driscoll was a master of the dropkick, a superb punter, and a shifty runner. While Halas organized the Staleys in Decatur and founded the league in 1920, Driscoll became the league's first franchise player with the Cardinals. Halas finally landed him for the Grange tour in 1925. Driscoll retired as a player after the 1929 season.

Driscoll had been the Bears' backfield coach since 1941, had never made strategic or tactical decisions, and unlike Halas, was soft-spoken and as gentle as a baby cub. He inherited a team that went 8–4 in 1955, finishing second by a half game behind the Los Angeles Rams in the renamed Western Division. Deep and talented at every position, with the top offense in the league led by quarterback Ed Brown, MVP end Harlon Hill, and fullback Rick Casares, the Bears were preseason favorites to win the NFL title in 1956.

Such players as Harlon Hill and Rick Casares said the quiet, amiable Driscoll stood sentry on the sidelines in

1956 and 1957, while Halas, in reality, called the shots as always. On February 16, 1958, Papa Bear announced that he was returning to action and giving his friend Paddy Driscoll an impressive but empty title: administrative vice president— another way of saying that Driscoll's sole duty was to watch game movies. However, Halas was instrumental in getting his old friend elected to the Pro Football Hall of Fame in 1965. Driscoll died in 1968 at age 73.

George Halas and Paddy Driscoll were players for the Bears when this photo was taken in 1926. Driscoll started on the rival Cardinals team before Halas recruited him for the Grange tour in 1925.

CHICAGO BEARS
NATIONAL CHAMPIONS
~ 1940 ~

The Monsters of the Midway routed the Washington Redskins 73-0 on December 8, 1940, to give the Bears their fourth title. Pictured here is the 1940 national champions team.

This program honors the 310 NFL players in the service—many of the Bears' greatest stars were among them. The Redskins upset the unbeaten Bears 14-6 to gain revenge for their 73-0 defeat in the 1940 title game.

WORLD'S CHAMPIONSHIP
NATIONAL FOOTBALL LEAGUE
DEC. 13,   1942
PLAYERS IN THE

310

ARMED SERVICES

CHAMPIONS
of the West
CHICAGO BEARS
vs.
CHAMPIONS
of the East
WASHINGTON REDSKINS

GRIFFITH STADIUM, WASHINGTON, D.C.
OFFICIAL MAGAZINE   •   PRICE 10c

The dangerous Packers gave their old rivals all they could handle on November 3, 1946, at Wrigley Field. The Bears eked out a 10-7 victory.

BEARS VS. PACKERS

WRIGLEY FIELD · NOVEMBER 3, 1946
Official Program 25¢

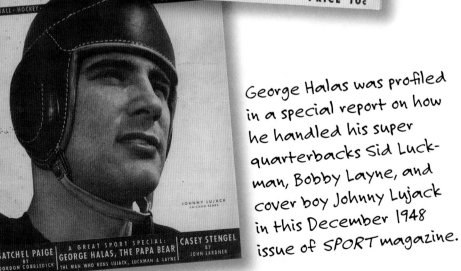

SPORT
BASKETBALL · HOCKEY

JOHNNY LUJACK
CHICAGO BEARS

SATCHEL PAIGE
BY
GORDON COBBLEDICK

A GREAT SPORT SPECIAL:
GEORGE HALAS, THE PAPA BEAR
THE MAN WHO RUNS LUJACK, LUCKMAN & LAYNE

CASEY STENGEL
BY
JOHN LARDNER

George Halas was profiled in a special report on how he handled his super quarterbacks Sid Luckman, Bobby Layne, and cover boy Johnny Lujack in this December 1948 issue of SPORT magazine.

Riddell produced this metal sign to honor the 1946 champion Bears. Sporting goods dealers across the country put it on display.

BEARS

CHICAGO BEARS

WORLD CHAMPIONS

1946

Riddell

PROTECTING GREAT TEAMS SINCE 1929

In 1946, George Halas wrote this recruiting letter to Hank Foldberg, the Army All-America end who still had a year left at West Point. Foldberg played two years in the AAFC.

WRIGLEY FIELD, HOME OF THE BEARS

CHICAGO BEARS FOOTBALL CLUB
INCORPORATED

NATIONAL CHAMPIONS 1921-1932-1933-1940-1941-1943
WESTERN CHAMPIONS 1934-1937-1942

GEO. S. HALAS
President-Treasurer

J. W. McMILLEN
Vice-President

WALTER H. HALAS
Vice-President

R. D. BRIZZOLARA
Secretary

27 SOUTH WABASH AVENUE
CHICAGO 3, ILLINOIS
November 25, 1946

Telephone
FRAnklin 6040

Mr. Henry Foldberg
U. S. Military Academy
West Point, New York

Dear Mr. Foldberg:

It is my understanding that you are about to complete your college career and your college athletic eligibility this year. Since plans for our club are now being formulated for the next football season, I would like to know if you would be interested in playing with the Chicago Bears next fall.

In the event you are not finishing school now, I should like to urge you to continue your college education and your college athletic competition. If you are terminating your college career, I should like to have an opportunity to discuss your plans for the future with you. I am confident that you would fit into our club.

Whether or not you are continuing your college work, it would be appreciated if you would fill out the enclosed questionaire and return it to me in the enclosed, self-addressed envelope.

Cordially yours,

Geo. Halas
President.

GSH:nmm

The December 1957 cover of SPORT magazine featured Rick Casares and Stan Jones—Bears who could lead the new Monsters to a title.

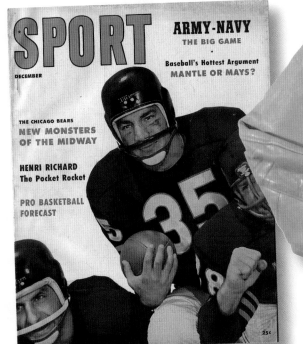

SPORT

DECEMBER

ARMY-NAVY
THE BIG GAME

Baseball's Hottest Argument
MANTLE OR MAYS?

THE CHICAGO BEARS
NEW MONSTERS
OF THE MIDWAY

HENRI RICHARD
The Pocket Rocket

PRO BASKETBALL
FORECAST

25¢

CHICAGO BEARS

The Chicago Bears version of a letterman's jacket was popular in the 1950s with high school and college athletic teams.

THE TEAM THAT SHOULD HAVE WON IT ALL

The 1956 Bears had everything, including future Hall of Famers Doug Atkins, Bill George, George Blanda, and Stan Jones. Also present were Harlon Hill and Rick Casares, who should have been Hall of Famers as well. The Bears had the league's best offense, and the defense was hostile, mobile, and agile. And though heavily favored to win it all, they failed miserably.

The Baltimore Colts stole a 28–21 opening-week victory with a brilliant play by quarterback George Shaw. That roused the Bears, who averaged 38 points per game through the next

Johnny Lujack (32) and Sid Luckman (42) are shown together in 1949. Lujack, the heir apparent, took over as starting quarterback, and he led the NFL with 2,568 passing yards and 23 touchdown passes. Lujack's abrupt retirement at the end of 1951, after four seasons, derailed a potential Hall of Fame career.

The Bears—the Western Division champs—led by NFL rushing champion Rick Casares (second from left), charge onto Yankee Stadium's field for a final practice on Saturday, December 19, 1956, before the next day's title game with the New York Giants.

seven contests. The big explosion came in game four, when they routed the Colts 58–27 after knocking Shaw out for the season with a knee injury. Shaw's replacement, rookie Johnny Unitas, threw the first pass of his career, but J. C. Caroline intercepted it and returned it 59 yards for a Bears touchdown.

A showdown came in New York on November 25 with the Eastern-leading Giants. Tom Landry's defense throttled Rick Casares, the league's leading rusher at the time. Vince Lombardi's offense built a 17–3 lead with five minutes left, but Luke Johnsos had seen enough; he called for a gadget

Sneakers-clad Dick Yelvington (72) leads Alex Webster (Giants 29) on a sure-footed run past Fred Williams (75), Ed Meadows (86), John Helwig (80), and McNeil Moore (Bears 29) to a 47–7 New York Giants rout of the Bears for the 1956 title at Yankee Stadium.

play that dated all the way back to 1933. Bill McColl took Ed Brown's handoff from his end position, but instead of tucking the ball and running with it, he fired downfield and hit Harlon Hill in stride for a 79-yard touchdown pass to make it 17–10. McColl's end-around throw caught everyone on New York's defense by surprise.

Then, with less than a minute to go, Brown dropped back from the Bears' 44-yard line and fired to Hill, who made an incredible juggling grab with his fingertips in the end zone for another improbable score. The Bears escaped with a 17–17 tie.

Unfortunately, disaster followed in a 42–10 blowout loss to the Lions in Detroit. Then the next week, the Bears barely survived with a 10–3 win over the Cardinals in a brawl-marred battle. A week later, after Ed Meadows knocked Bobby Layne

from the game, the Bears routed the Lions 38–21. Casares ran for a team-record 190 yards to finish as the league's top ground-gainer with 1,126 yards.

While the Giants took a break over the Christmas holiday, Halas kept the Bears working every day—most of the time in full pads. The Bears were edgy on December 30 when they took to the Yankee Stadium field with short rubber cleats. The Giants were relaxed and ready, and because the field had frozen, they wore sneakers as they had back in 1934. Gene Filipski returned the opening kickoff to the Bears' 38, with Mel Triplett scoring two plays later. The Giants raced to a 34–7 halftime lead and coasted home to take the title 47–7. It was the second time Halas and the Bears beat themselves with shoddy preparation and improper footwear.

PAPA BEAR RETURNS

After the 1957 season, when George Halas finally admitted to himself that he had to consign Paddy Driscoll to the trash heap, he decided to turn the team over to the one man who could make it win: himself. So, on February 16, 1958, George Halas announced that he was returning to coach his 31st National Football League season. And he let it be known that he intended to win.

It started with a somewhat retooled staff. Loyal to a fault to the men who had been with him for years—men such as Driscoll, Luke Johnsos, line coach Phil Handler, Clark Shaughnessy, and now defensive coach and dollar-a-year quarterback coach Sid Luckman—the Old Man knew he needed fresh, contemporary ideas and someone to install organization into his operation.

Two young career coaches joined the staff in 1958. Chuck Mather was a disciple of Paul Brown in Massillon, Ohio, where he broke his mentor's high school coaching records. Mather arrived from the University of Kansas, where he was Big 8 Coach of the Year in 1957. Halas asked Mather to modernize offensive techniques and write a playbook to be given to each player. Previously, players had to memorize the plays drawn up on shirt cardboards held up in front of the team by a coach.

Halas also hired George Allen, a former assistant with the Los Angeles Rams. Allen wore two hats: personnel director in charge of the draft and defensive assistant to Shaughnessy.

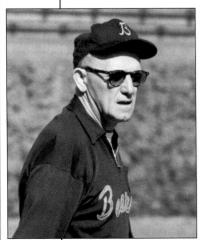

George Halas returned to the sidelines in 1958 for his fourth term as head coach. He won his sixth and last title in 1963 at age 68. He was also named Coach of the Year twice: once in 1963 and again in '65 before his 1968 retirement.

TRAINER ANDY LOTSHAW

The Bears team was overflowing with characters, but one of the most beloved was colorful trainer Andy Lotshaw. Lotshaw, a former minor league ballplayer, joined George Halas in Decatur in 1920, moved with him to Chicago, and remained with the Bears until 1947. Though he had no formal education, Lotshaw used his Andy Lotshaw's Body Rub ("It could cure anything") to knead aching muscles during football season and sore arms and legs during baseball season.

After leaving the Bears, "Doc" Lotshaw hung on with the Cubs until 1952 before he went home to Indianapolis that winter and died at age 73. He can be found in all the Bears championship team photos from 1920 through their seventh title in 1946.

Andy Lotshaw was the Bears first trainer. He remained with the team for almost 30 years.

The effect was immediate, especially in Mather's case. The 1958 Bears had a strong opening in their first five games, losing only to the Colts in Baltimore. Both Rick Casares and second-year back Willie Galimore had fine seasons, and the team finished 8–4, second behind the Colts, who would go on to win the title at New York in football's first sudden-death overtime.

A 1958 milestone included the postseason departure of quarterback and place-kicker George Blanda at age 31; he was not satisfied with only being a kicker. Halas had no kicking replacement, so by forcing Blanda into retirement, Halas basically cut off his nose to spite his face. Blanda was the team's all-time leading scorer, with 541 points gained through 247 extra points and 88 field goals, plus 48 touchdown passes and five rushing touchdowns.

GAME DAY: 1959

By 1959, the Bears had rebounded from the 1956 title game debacle and a 1957 letdown that ended Paddy Driscoll's brief term as head coach. They were now positioned to challenge the world champion Baltimore Colts and their superstar quarterback, Johnny Unitas.

Entering their 40th season, the Bears were established as the National Football League's dominant team with seven world championships, ten Western Division titles, and 312 regular season victories, plus one divisional playoff and five title-game victories. They had scored 8,500 regular season points, plus 292 more in postseason play. Halas-coached teams had won 244 regular season games and 326 overall, including postseason and exhibitions.

During this time, a six-game season ticket book sold for $30 in the box seats and $24 in the bleachers. In 1947, Ralph Brizzolara designed a wooden and steel bleacher section that ran from the center-field wall to the right-field foul line. Extending upward 70 rows, the intimate seating pattern increased Wrigley Field's football capacity to 50,000 from baseball's 35,000. At season's end, the extra seats were dismantled and stored below the right-field bleachers.

Sundays at Wrigley Field during football season were quite an event. Women wore suits, weather-appropriate coats, and dress hats. During October and early November, almost all the men sported fedoras and wore sportcoats over neckties and sweaters with wool slacks. The storm coats and boots came out with the arrival of harsh wintry days in December.

At home, the Bears emerged from their locker room by the left-field corner wearing the navy blue—almost black—jersey with orange sleeve stripes, white pants with a blue horizontal stripe down the legs, navy blue stockings with orange horizontal stripes, and the plain navy helmet without insignia. The "C" on the helmet wouldn't be implemented until 1962. On the road, they wore white jerseys with navy blue numbers and orange and blue sleeve stripes.

The real show, however, began when Papa Bear took the field. Impeccably dressed in a dark suit and constantly tugging at the brim of his fedora, he was a part of the action when play began—he raced up and down the sidelines, taunting officials and opponents alike. Despite the tough crew of mugs and thugs he had at his disposal, Halas himself was the star of the show. What a sight it was.

The Bears called Wrigley Field home for 50 years (1921–1970), winning eight of their nine championships there. For football, the ballpark held as many as 50,000 fans thanks to Ralph Brizzolara's massive temporary bleachers across center and right fields.

STARS OF THE MONSTERS ERA

The era from 1940 through George Halas's final 1963 championship produced five titles and some of the greatest and most colorful players in league history.

Clyde "Bulldog" Turner arrived from tiny Hardin-Simmons University as the top draft choice in 1940 and anchored four NFL title teams in 13 stellar seasons. He set a league record with a 96-yard interception return in 1947 against Washington. An incredible two-way force, teammate George Musso once said of Turner, "Who knows what kind of player he would have been if he ever got to rest during a game?"

The second-overall choice in the 1940 NFL Draft, halfback **George "One Play" McAfee** hailed from Duke. Halas called McAfee the greatest game-breaker he'd ever coached until Hall of Famer Gale Sayers arrived from Kansas in 1965. One of the more versatile Bears to ever put on a uniform, he scored touchdowns five different ways in 1941 alone: six rushing, three receiving, and one each on a punt return, a kickoff return, and an interception return.

Bill George joined the Bears as a middle guard in 1952. Tall, quick, smart, and the defensive quarterback, he pretty much invented the middle linebacker position in 1954. Up until then, players at his position crashed the line of scrimmage and were often beaten with quick dump passes over the middle. George began to drop back from the line of scrimmage, and suddenly he was intercepting and knocking down throws left and right. The 4-3 defense, as we have come to know it, was born.

Hall of Fame quarterback and kicker **George Blanda** was drafted by the Bears in 1949. Halas "retired" Blanda after the 1958 season. Nonetheless, Blanda revived his career in 1960 at age 33 and lasted 16 more seasons in the American Football League and NFL with the Houston Oilers and Oakland Raiders.

Bill George dropped back from his middle guard position against the Eagles in 1953 and snatched the first of his 18 career interceptions. Soon, he lined up in the middle behind the line, inventing the middle linebacker position that turned him into a Hall of Famer.

George Blanda was "retired" when he refused to become only a kicker for the 1959 season. He went on to play for the Oilers and the Raiders, becoming the oldest quarterback to play in a championship game in the AFC when the Raiders played the Colts in 1971.

Tight end Mike Ditka justified his selection as NFL Rookie of the Year in 1961, and he earned All-Pro honors four times through 1966. This future Hall of Famer left due to a money dispute with George Halas; however, Halas hired him as the Bears head coach in 1982. Ditka became a Super Bowl winner in 1985.

Two more Hall of Famers included guard/tackle **Stan Jones** and the team's first true tight end, **Mike Ditka.** Jones is believed to be the first pro footballer to make lifting weights a part of his regular routine, a practice that was previously frowned upon for fear of limited mobility and flexibility. He played for the Bears from 1954 through 1965. Ditka was the league's Rookie of the Year in 1961, twice an All-Pro and an offensive captain in Chicago through 1966. Despite all that, he punched a ticket to Philadelphia in '67 when he accused George Halas of tossing around nickels like manhole covers. In 1969, he joined the Dallas Cowboys, with whom he finished his playing career in '72. Ditka next began a coaching career that would bring him home to Chicago in 1982 to restore the franchise to glory.

George Connor came from Notre Dame in 1948. He made All-Pro at tackle before a twist of fate in 1949. The Eagles were killing the Chicago defense, with Steve Van Buren being led through wide-open holes by his fullback and two pulling guards. The Bears needed a bigger, faster player to help plug the holes—Connor got the call. The Bears defeated the Eagles 38–21, and Connor found a new home. He retired after the 1955 season at age 30.

Rick Casares joined the Bears in 1955, becoming the team's greatest fullback since Bronko Nagurski.

Fullback Rick Casares from Florida joined the Bears in 1955 and stayed through 1964. He led the league in 1956 with 1,146 yards. He remains third on the team's all-time ground gaining list with 5,675 yards, behind Walter Payton and Neal Anderson.

George Connor (71) executes a smashing stiff arm against a Los Angeles Ram on this 17-yard run with a recovered fumble. Connor's Hall of Fame career at tackle and linebacker lasted from 1948 to 1955.

The nightlife-loving Casares led the NFL in 1956 with 1,126 yards rushing. He retired after ten seasons as the franchise's all-time leading rusher with 5,675 yards on the ground before his totals were surpassed by Walter Payton.

Harlon Hill, a 6′3″, 200-pound split end, arrived from Florence State Teachers College in 1954. The league's MVP in 1955, Hill injured his back in the 1956 title game and never recaptured the magic he had earlier in his career. Still, he averaged an astounding 20.4 yards per catch in his eight years with the Bears.

Harlon Hill arrived from the tiny Florence Alabama State Teachers College to make All-Pro from 1954 to 1956. Unfortunately, injuries curtailed his career, and it ended in 1962. Tall, fast, and tough, he was the prototype modern receiver.

BEST OF THE BEARS

The Midwest Shrine Game is a Packer tradition; they donate a percentage of the gate to the Shriners Hospitals for Children. At this game versus the Bears, Vince Lombardi's defending-champion Packers coasted to a 35-21 victory.

This media guide features a team on a mission. They win the Bears' eighth title!

The 1963 world champion Bears are honored on this plaque that lists team scores and players.

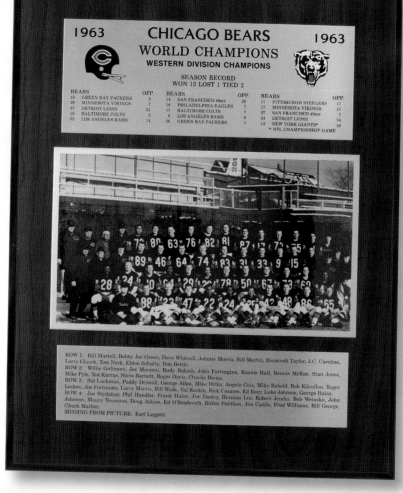

This Press Guide honors the team's eight world championships. The 1964 Bears broke down, however, and ended with a 5-9 record.

The Bears opened their 32nd season at City Stadium with a 31-20 victory over the Packers. The early promise ended with a disappointing 7-5 record.

Official Program

PITTSBURGH STEELERS
OCTOBER 7
(Milwaukee)

CHICAGO BEARS
SEPTEMBER 30
(City Stadium)

CHICAGO BEARS
vs.
GREEN BAY PACKERS

PHILADELPHIA EAGLES
OCTOBER 14
(City Stadium)

LOS ANGELES RAMS
OCTOBER 27
(Milwaukee)

DETROIT LIONS
NOVEMBER 4
(City Stadium)

NEW YORK YANKS

SEPTEMBER 30, 1951
CITY STADIUM

Bobbleheads are popular collector's items; this one portrays a Chicago boy's dream—to be a Chicago Bear.

This helmet was autographed by the 1963 world champion Bears. George Halas's coaching brought Chicago their eighth title when they beat the New York Giants 14-10 at an icy Wrigley Field.

Clyde Turner writes about how to play the linebacker position effectively in his 1948 book, Playing the Line.

PLAYING THE LINE
by "Bulldog" Turner

LITTLE SPORTS LIBRARY $1.25

1963: A BEAR MARKET

After Green Bay's 1962 victory party to honor coach Vince Lombardi, George Halas came home to Chicago and told his coaches that his Bears would "beat that &$*#&#&&#" in the fall. The determined Halas then ordered offensive assistant Chuck Mather to select a short list of plays designed to beat Green Bay. Halas had turned over the defense to assistant George Allen in late 1962, and Allen cut his defense loose. He relied on a heavy pass rush, blitzes, and tight man-to-man pass defense. Mather pared down the offense to a tough, ball-possession ground game and a sharp, short-passing attack built around flanker Johnny Morris and the best tight end in the business, Mike Ditka. For good measure, he made Ditka an offensive co-captain with center Mike Pyle to complement new defensive captain Joe Fortunato. In April, a stroke of luck came for the Bears when Commissioner Pete

Rozelle lowered the boom on their closest rivals when he suspended the Packers' star halfback, Paul Hornung, and Lions defensive tackle Alex Karras, for betting on games. All of the Bears' hard work paid off in a 10–3 opening-game victory at Green Bay as the Bears intercepted five Bart Starr passes, allowed just 150 total yards, and never let the Packers get closer than the Chicago 33-yard line. Halas had a game ball made up that remains on display at Halas Hall in Lake Forest with the pithy comment, "Greatest team effort."

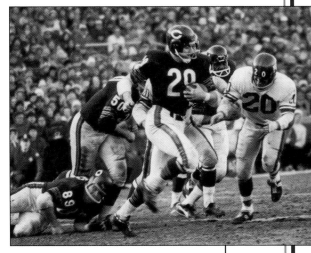

Halfback Ronnie Bull (with the ball) gains tough yards against New York's Jimmy Patton (20) with help from Mike Ditka (89, on the ground) and Mike Pyle (50) in the 1963 championship game at Wrigley Field. The Bears, in proper footwear, beat the Giants 14–10 to claim the team's eighth title.

Then, on November 17 at the Packer rematch at Wrigley Field, the most ballyhooed regular season game in league history, the Bears put on a show for the ages. It started on the opening kickoff when J. C. Caroline flattened Green Bay returner Herb Adderley at his own 20 to set the stage. After the second of two Roger LeClerc field goals, John Farrington ripped the resulting kickoff from Adderley's hands. Three plays later, Willie Galimore, who had just recovered from double knee surgery, slashed to the outside, hurdled blocker Ditka, and sped 27 yards to the end zone, making the score 13–0 Bears in the first quarter. The Packers were finished as the Bears romped to victory 26–7.

THREE FOR THE HALL

Pro football was the last major sport to establish a Hall of Fame. Commissioner Pete Rozelle opened the doors to the Canton, Ohio, shrine on George Halas Drive to induct the charter class. Three Bears were among the 17 chosen by hall electors. These 17 carried the National Football League from its 1920 founding to the television era and included founder/player/owner/coach George Halas; the man who first brought the game to the attention of the nation, Harold "Red" Grange; and the man who exemplified the game's toughness and indomitable will, Bronko Nagurski. Twenty-six men have been inducted as Bears, plus five more who once played for the team. No franchise has more.

HOORAY FOR HALAS AND ALLEN

Chicagoans, at 45,000 strong, braved arctic weather on Sunday, December 29, 1963, to see the championship showdown between the Bears and the New York Giants at frozen Wrigley Field. With the game blacked out in Chicago, another 26,000 jammed into three arenas—McCormick Place, the International Amphitheatre, and Chicago Coliseum—for a closed-circuit telecast. Unlike the 1934 and 1956 disasters, George Halas outfitted his troops in proper footwear.

The Giants led 7–0 when Y. A. Tittle cashed in on a Billy Wade fumble and then connected with Frank Gifford for a 14-yard scoring pass. After a Willie Galimore fumble, New York went in for the kill, but Del Shofner dropped Tittle's bomb in the end zone.

George Allen and Jim Dooley had schooled the Bear defense on Giants' plays. When Larry Morris saw Tittle look to his right, he knew Tittle would throw a screen left. Morris, *SPORT* magazine's Most Valuable Player, reacted, intercepted, and chugged downfield 60 yards to the New York 6-yard line. Wade scored on a quarterback sneak behind the wedge blocking of center Mike Pyle and left guard Ted Karras to tie it 7–7.

In the second quarter, Morris twisted Tittle's left knee as he planted his foot, forcing him to the sideline. A less agile Tittle returned after two halftime novocaine shots. Late in the third quarter, Tittle tried a screen to his right. Defensive left end Ed O'Bradovich read the play, intercepted the pass, and lumbered to the Giants' 14. Luke Johnsos called a down-and-in pass—Wade to Mike Ditka, who got to the one. Wade scored a play later on the sneak for a 14–10 Bears lead.

The defense closed out the Bears' eighth championship, the sixth for Coach Halas. In the locker room, the team awarded the game ball to George Allen, singing, "Hooray for George, hooray at last. Hooray for George, he's a horse's ass!" The assistant promptly handed the ball to his boss.

The Bears staff, (left to right) Abe Gibron, Jim Dooley, Phil Handler, Chuck Mather, George Allen, Ed Cody, George Halas, and Luke Johnsos, gathers for a meeting in the Film Room on 173 W. Madison Street in 1965. George Allen was the personnel director and assistant coach at the time.

CHAPTER THREE

THE MERGER ERA

1964–1981

"Ed—Players play. Coaches coach. Scouts scout. General managers manage. And owners own. Now, Ed, go own!"

GENERAL MANAGER JIM FINKS TELLS REPORTERS HOW HE HANDLED HALAS SON-IN-LAW ED MCCASKEY, CIRCA 1975

Above: *This pin proclaims that the Bears are the NFL's oldest team.* **Right:** *In his first NFL start, rookie Gale Sayers (40) uses blocks from Johnny Morris (47) and Mike Ditka (89) to burst through the Packers line for a big gain at Lambeau Field on October 3, 1965. His two touchdowns weren't enough, however—Green Bay won 23–14.*

DICK BUTKUS

To this day, wherever you go, wherever the game is played, the name Dick Butkus instantly connotes Chicago and football. This native South Sider, a proud alumnus of the University of Illinois and the ultimate Bear, was ferocious, tough, and unconquerable.

By the time he graduated, 22-year-old Butkus knew he was going home to play for the Bears. He had money in the bank thanks to the deal that the legendary lawyer/sports promoter Arthur Morse cut with George Halas. In the years prior to 1965, Halas had negotiated with agents for only two players,

Rookie and All-Pro Dick Butkus (51) bats down a Johnny Unitas (19) pass at Wrigley Field on November 7, 1965. Despite Butkus's heroic play, the Baltimore Colts beat the Bears 26–21. The loss ended a four-game winning streak for Chicago.

Red Grange and George Connor. Butkus became the third because he was just that exceptional. Morse walked away with a five-year deal worth an unprecedented $200,000—solid money, no qualifiers, no incentives.

Middle linebacker Butkus was unquestionably the top defensive player in the country when Illinois won the Rose Bowl in 1963 and again in 1964. Also in 1964, he finished third in Heisman Trophy balloting behind two quarterbacks, John Huarte from Notre Dame and Jerry Rhome from Tulsa.

> TO THIS DAY, WHEREVER YOU GO, WHEREVER THE GAME IS PLAYED, THE NAME DICK BUTKUS INSTANTLY CONNOTES CHICAGO AND FOOTBALL.

The Bears' Bill George—a future Hall of Famer who had invented the middle linebacker position—knew he was finished the moment he saw Butkus take charge during practice in the summer of 1965 in Rensselaer, Indiana. Butkus went on to be named to the 1965 NFL All-Pro team (legendary Packer linebacker Ray Nitschke was not) and also earned NFL Defensive Rookie of the Year honors. By 1971, when Butkus grew a fearsome mustache and sold his likeness for the wrapper of the Super Crunch candy bar, he was regarded as the NFL's all-time best middle linebacker. He still is.

Sadly, the Bears never made the playoffs in Butkus's nine years. In the 1970–71 off-season, Bears physician Dr. Ted Fox performed surgery on Butkus's right knee

Dick Butkus is ready to spring into action—the name Butkus remains synonymous with defense. Once called "the greatest Bear of all" by George Halas, Butkus dominated the league for nine seasons and was All-Pro for seven of those years.

to tighten ligaments; the knee was never the same. When Butkus signed a five-year series of one-year contracts in 1973 for $115,000 a year, Halas did not make him take a physical. Butkus would have flunked it—by then, his right leg at the knee joint was bone on bone.

By 1973, Butkus needed help to get dressed. He could barely walk and couldn't practice. In the ninth game of the season, an ABC Monday nighter at Kansas City, Butkus could not come out for the second half. He never played again.

This end to Butkus's career led to one of the nastiest public disputes in NFL history. Certain that Papa Bear would not honor the star's contract because he was injured, Butkus sued George Halas, his boss and idol, in 1975.

Butkus's lawyer, noted personal injury attorney James Dooley, discovered an ironclad Arthur Morse–stipulated clause in Butkus's original contract that guaranteed payment to his client regardless of injury. In 1976, on the recommendation of his attorney, Don Reuben, who knew the severity of the damage, Halas settled with Butkus for $600,000.

Regardless of their past, Butkus stood in line in 1979 for Halas to autograph a copy of his autobiography, *Halas by Halas.* In the inscription the old coach wrote, "To Dick Butkus, the greatest player in the history of the Bears, You had that old Zipperoo."

Halas, though, had set a mousetrap for himself. He wanted to retire the number 40 that was worn by his personal favorite, Gale Sayers. Yet Sayers and Butkus were so identified as teammates and best-in-league-history at their positions, Halas could not honor Sayers unless he also retired the defiant Butkus's number 51. As long as Halas lived, those two numbers remained unretired.

DICK BUTKUS AND HIS HIGH-IMPACT NUMBERS

Dick Butkus appeared in eight Pro Bowls from 1965 through 1972. He was a first-team selection on at least one All-Pro team in every season he played and earned consensus first-team all-NFL honors five times: in 1965, 1968, 1969, 1970, and 1972.

Butkus recovered 6 fumbles as a rookie, part of a franchise-record 27 for his career, and in 1973, he ran back a fumble 38 yards for a touchdown. He intercepted 22 passes, including a career-high 5 as a rookie. He even caught one memorable pass against the Washington Redskins at Soldier Field in 1971, when holder Bobby Douglass picked up a bad snap and threw a pass to a corner of the north end zone. Butkus caught it for the extra point in a 16–15 Bears victory.

He was inducted into the Pro Football Hall of Fame in 1979, and his number 51 was finally retired by the Bears in 1994.

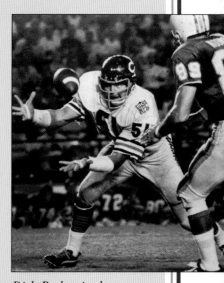

Dick Butkus is about to make an interception, helping the Bears beat the Dolphins 16–10 in an exhibition game on August 9, 1969, at the Orange Bowl in Miami. Butkus was All-Pro for a team that went 1–13.

GALE SAYERS: THE KANSAS COMET

George Halas knew he was in for a tough battle in the winter of 1965, when he had to outbid Kansas City Chiefs owner Lamar Hunt of the rival AFL to sign running back Gale Sayers. Papa Bear was desperate to land Sayers when he saw his game films from the University of Kansas. The last runner Halas had seen of equal talent was George "One Play" McAfee, the Hall of Fame breakaway star of the Monsters of the Midway dynasty.

When Sayers visited Chicago, Halas told him to go back to Hunt and get his best offer, then return. Halas landed Sayers for four years for $100,000. Forty years later, Sayers admitted he took a chance, but added, "I'm glad I played for a man like George Halas."

The feeling was mutual, and for 68 games, the thrills and excitement were unending every time the 6'0", 198-pound Sayers, the fourth pick overall in the 1965 NFL draft, stepped on a field wearing number 40 in the Chicago Bears colors. Sayers got his first start in game three in 1965 at Green Bay, playing with fellow rookie Dick Butkus, a linebacker. Sayers scored two touchdowns in the second half as Vince Lombardi's Packers escaped with a 23–14 win. The next time they met Green Bay, on Halloween in Chicago, Sayers broke loose to lead the Bears to a 31–10 romp. That climaxed a spectacular month that saw him dazzle the Minnesota Vikings with four touchdowns, including a kickoff runback in a 45–37 thriller.

At New York's Yankee Stadium on November 28, Sayers came through with two long, twisting touchdown runs and a halfback option scoring pass to stun the Giants

35–14. Next was the masterpiece against the 49ers on December 12, in driving rain at Wrigley Field. Sayers broke loose for six touchdowns, the last was an 85-yard punt return to cap a 61–20 Bears romp. For the season, he scored a rookie-record 22 touchdowns for 132 points on 2,272 all-purpose yards.

The hits kept coming. He was the league leader in ground-gaining in 1966 and was on his way to a rushing title in 1968, when he tore his right knee ligaments in a hit by 49ers Kermit Alexander. After months of rehabilitation with Dick Woit at the Lawson YMCA in Chicago, Sayers returned in 1969 to lead the league in rushing. Injured in 1970, he tried one more comeback in 1971, then quit at age 28. At age 34, in 1977, he was the youngest man elected to the Hall of Fame. A tearful

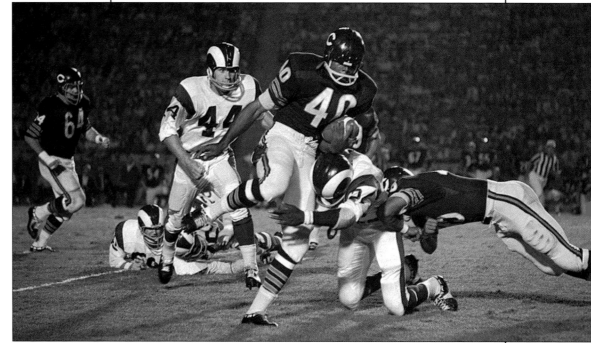

Gale Sayers (40) exhibits his great elusiveness in an exhibition game against the Los Angeles Rams on August 28, 1965, at the L.A. Coliseum; the Bears beat the Rams 28–14. Later, Sayers was named NFL Rookie of the Year.

Sayers went over to Halas after his introduction and kissed him on the cheek.

Sayers became an athletic administrator and served as athletic director at Southern Illinois. Then he returned to Chicago, where he founded Sayers Computer Source, an IT support firm that he still runs.

In 1994, Halas's grandson, Michael McCaskey, finally decided to retire Sayers's number 40 and Butkus's number 51. He slated the ceremony for Monday night, October 31. In a rainstorm that saw Green Bay run up a 33–6 halftime lead, fans saw Sayers and Butkus tour the field in a soaked convertible. More than one Chicagoan noted that the uniform retirements coincided with the death of George Halas, 11 years to the night.

Gale Sayers is caught in a swarm of New York Giants as the Bears overwhelm their ancient rivals 34–7 on November 12, 1967, at Wrigley Field.

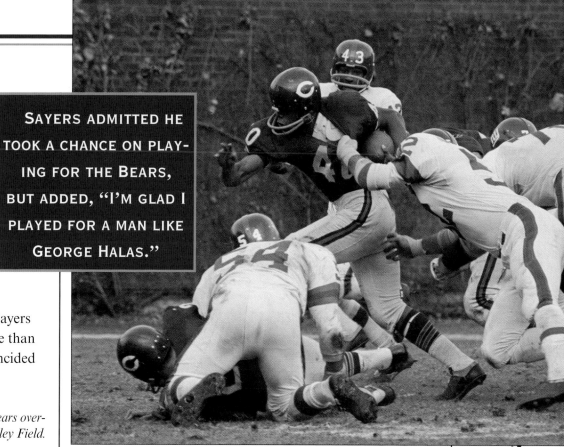

SAYERS ADMITTED HE TOOK A CHANCE ON PLAYING FOR THE BEARS, BUT ADDED, "I'M GLAD I PLAYED FOR A MAN LIKE GEORGE HALAS."

GALE SAYERS AND HIS HIGH-IMPACT NUMBERS

Like Gale Sayers's nickname, "the Kansas Comet," his career was bright and dazzling before it was doused by crippling injuries. It was so brief—just 68 effervescent games. When he took center stage, though, no athlete shone more radiantly.

His rookie year, 1965, set the course: 22 touchdowns on 14 runs, six pass receptions, one kickoff runback, and one punt return; he had 867 yards on the ground and 2,272 all-purpose yards. Sayers was also the league-leading rusher twice: in 1966 with 1,231 yards and in 1969 with 1,069 yards.

Overall, he had 56 career touchdowns, which includes 39 touchdown runs, nine touchdown receptions, two punt returns, and six kick returns, as well as one touchdown pass on a halfback option.

Sayers was inducted into the Pro Football Hall of Fame in 1977, and his number 40 was finally retired in 1994.

From left to right, Forrest Gregg, Frank Gifford, Gale Sayers, Bart Starr, and Bill Willis are inducted into the Pro Football Hall of Fame in Canton, Ohio, on July 30, 1977. Sayers is the youngest-ever inductee at age 34.

THE INSPIRATIONAL BRIAN PICCOLO

As the subject of two books and a made-for-TV classic, running back Brian Piccolo became a legend in his 26 years—his life was cut short by a rare form of testicular cancer. Piccolo, a 6'0", 205-pounder with average speed, was college football's leading ground-gainer in 1964 at Wake Forest. George Allen signed him as an undrafted free agent, and he became a starter in 1968 when Gale Sayers hurt his knee.

Piccolo took ill in October 1969 with a "flu-like cough." The doctors made the cancer diagnosis and sent him to Sloan-Kettering Hospital in New York for treatment. George Halas picked up all the medical costs.

Brian Piccolo (41), playing with the desire and spirit that typified him. Each year, the Bears honor a rookie and a veteran who have embodied that same drive.

BRIAN'S SONG

Few made-for-TV motion pictures have had a lasting impact as significant as *Brian's Song.* The film, which tells the story of cancer-stricken, white football player Brian Piccolo and his friendship with black teammate Gale Sayers, premiered on November 30, 1971, on ABC-TV. It won three Emmy Awards, has been rerun frequently on television, and is still used in school assemblies today to teach kids about seeing across racial lines and having courage when times are tough.

Brian's Song has remained popular for nearly four decades. The actors were superb: James Caan, who played Piccolo, also had a role as Sonny Corleone in *The Godfather,* which was set to be released in March 1972. Billy Dee Williams, who played the future Hall of Famer Sayers, was a rising star—a young, African American leading man destined for a long run on Hollywood's A-list. But the major reason the film has endured is its universal messages of black-and-white harmony, courageous determination, and unwavering compassion.

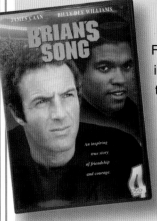

The award-winning Brian's Song *starred James Caan as Brian Piccolo and Billy Dee Williams as Brian's friend and roommate Gale Sayers.*

Piccolo's story caught notice when Al Silverman ghosted *I Am Third,* an autobiography of Gale Sayers. Piccolo and Sayers were roommates on road trips, and they got along quite well. Sayers dedicated a chapter of the book to Piccolo, which became the basis for the 1971 ABC-TV film *Brian's Song.*

When Piccolo took ill, Sayers and his other teammates rallied to his cause. "We cared about him," Sayers said in the biography *Papa Bear: The Life and Legacy of George Halas.* "He was part of our team. He helped us in victory. He helped us in defeat. That's what the movie brought out."

After his death on June 16, 1970, the Bears retired Piccolo's number 41 and continue to bestow annual awards on top rookies and most valuable players in his name. His widow, Joy Piccolo O'Connell, and their three daughters, who were small children at the time of his death, honor him with the Brian Piccolo Cancer Research Fund.

THE GREAT DEPARTURES OF 1967

George Allen left the Bears for the Los Angeles Rams in 1966, and he built his great L.A. and Washington teams around an "Over the Hill Gang" of Bear veterans. He took part of the 1963 championship team with him, including long-time captain, signal caller, and middle linebacker Bill George, defensive tackle Earl Leggett, and left guard Ted Karras. Hammond, Indiana, and Northwestern product George Burman, who became the NFL's first long-snap specialist, also left with Allen. Burman later gained academic distinction as dean of Syracuse University's Whitman School of Management.

In the 1966–67 off season, George Halas gave away two title mainstays to the New Orleans Saints in the expansion draft: cornerback Davey Whitsell, whose interception and 39-yard touchdown runback against the Lions put the Bears in the 1963 title game; and colorful Doug Atkins, Papa Bear's all-time favorite defensive end and late-night sparring partner in many a "cuss-fight."

Other '63 ring wearers who did not return in '67 were halfback "Jaguar" Jon Arnett, fullbacks Joe Marconi and Charlie Bivins, defensive tackle John Johnson, kicker/linebacker Roger LeClerc, veteran offensive left tackle Herman Lee, and the key offensive

Mike Ditka was one of the NFL's greatest tight ends, going All–Pro from 1961 to 1965. Eventually, George Halas traded him due to a money dispute.

player since 1961, tight end Mike Ditka, who Halas traded to Philadelphia.

Since then, the Bears have burned through scores of tight ends but have been left wanting. No one has ever replaced Ditka, the Hall of Famer who defined the position. The backbreaker in Ditka's quarrelsome relationship with the Old Man came when he decided to play out his option. Halas called this an act of betrayal, as Ditka cashed a $50,000 signing bonus check in the summer of 1966, from the Houston Oilers—a member of the rival AFL—as part of AFL commissioner Al Davis's plan to sign NFL stars. The AFL-NFL merger approval was announced a few days later, ending that and other league-jumping deals; however, Ditka was not required to give back the money, and he didn't.

Thus Halas—in accordance with the league agreement on a player's exercising the option clause—cut Ditka's salary by ten percent. Then, in the fall of a dismal 5–7–2 1966 season, Ditka sealed his fate when he did not deny the oft-quoted wisecrack that Halas threw nickels around like manhole covers. As a result, in early 1967, Ditka went into exile in Philly in exchange for quarterback Jack Concannon.

JIM DOOLEY GETS THE IMPOSSIBLE-TO-FILL CALL

By 1968, time had caught up with coach George Halas, now 73. His wife, Min, had died two years before. Bedeviled with a chronic hip injury that could be relieved only by a replacement operation, he could no longer roam the sidelines. On May 27, 1968, the old coach called a news conference to announce his retirement. His successor would be 38-year-old defensive coordinator and former offensive end Jim Dooley.

Dooley, an X's and O's genius, had designed the 1963 championship defense for George Allen and had come up with his own innovative schemes for 1965's league-leading offense. His efforts seemed to be working. But as Dooley recalled years later for the biography *Papa Bear: The Life and Legacy of George Halas,* Halas called him to his apartment the night of May 26 and presented the young assistant coach with an offer, take-it-or-leave-it: five years at $35,000 a year—no bonus and no outside income, which included commercials, radio, and

Jim Dooley was the top player choice for the Bears in 1952. He ended his playing career in 1962 to become the Bears' assistant coach and then was the head coach from 1968 to 1971.

the television show that augmented George Allen's salary as an assistant. Dooley knew he would lose the opportunity if he balked, so he accepted Halas's offer.

Dooley, unfortunately, had two major weaknesses. He was a plunger at the racetrack, a big money loser; worse, he could not handle his players, and they knew it. After a 7–7 season, in 1968, with the team falling a game short of the playoffs, everything unraveled. Despite the All-Pro presence of Gale Sayers and Dick Butkus, the Bears went 1–13 in 1969.

After a late-season collapse in 1971 that caused the team to lose its final five games and end at 6–8, Halas reluctantly fired Dooley. Dooley roamed the football wilderness for a decade until Halas called and asked him to rejoin the staff. Dooley, rehabilitated and grateful, came back to do what he did best—break down film and help plan.

HALAS NAMED PRESIDENT OF THE NFC

The National Football League merger with the American Football League, announced in the summer of 1966, took effect in 1970. To honor the founder of the league, the 13 teams that comprised the new National Football Conference (NFC) named George Halas president.

The title was honorary for the most part, but the NFC, as well as the whole league, was able to benefit from the founder's 50 years of experience and wisdom in all matters. The league named its championship trophy (awarded each year to the NFC champion and Super Bowl representative) the George S. Halas Trophy. Two of these trophies—for the 1985 and 2006 seasons—adorn the Bears' trophy case at Halas Hall in Lake Forest, Illinois.

50 YEARS AT WRIGLEY

THE BEARS SAY GOODBYE

On December 13, 1970, the Bears beat the Green Bay Packers 35–17 to finish their home season at Wrigley Field. It was the last time they would play in the only Chicago home they had ever known since George Halas brought the Staleys to town in 1921.

Still alive and well as the home of baseball's Cubs, the Friendly Confines has played host to 342 pro football games. The Bears played 332 of their games there: 330 as the home team for 50 seasons from 1921 to 1970 and two more as visitors in 1920, when they were based in Decatur. Their record at Wrigley Field is 221–89–22, including victories in all four title games played. Now *that* was a home-field advantage!

Wrigley Field is wonderful as baseball's cathedral, but it was every bit as marvelous for Chicago Bears football, as shown here in 1939.

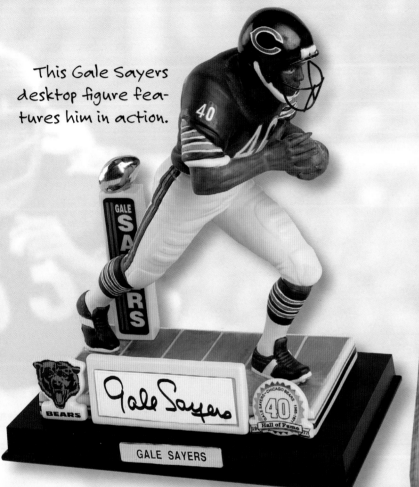

This Gale Sayers desktop figure features him in action.

This banner honored Gale Sayers as the 1965 NFL Rookie of the Year. Note that the autograph is from 1977, the year he was inducted into the Pro Football Hall of Fame.

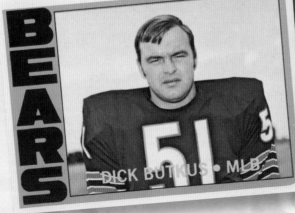

This 1972 Topps trading card portrays Dick Butkus—one of the greatest linebackers of all time.

As noted by columnist Bill Gleason, Paddy Driscoll was honored by his alma mater, Northwestern University, a few weeks after his induction into the Pro Football Hall of Fame. A close friend of George Halas, Driscoll was the Bears' head coach during the 1956 and 1957 seasons.

Dick Butkus autographed his number 51 jersey.

"PADDY DRISCOLL DAY" ·· August, 25, 1965

CHICAGO'S AMERICAN, THURSDAY, AUGUST 26, 1965

43

Bill Gleason

'N' Men Honor Driscoll, Find Time to See 'Purple'

WHEREVER HE appeared, Paddy Driscoll drew a crowd. Whether it was in Evanston's Mason park, or old Normal park stadium, or a semi-pro field in Hammond or Wrigley field, the people came out to see Paddy. And they're still coming out.

There wasn't a vacant space in the parking lot of the Wilmette Golf club last night where members of Northwestern university's "N" Men's club assembled to honor the wispy, little gaffer who is Chicago's No. 1 sports immortal.

This was an all day thing, with golf during the afternoon and dinner at night, but the guys who made the trip weren't there to play golf. They were there to unanimously indorse the words of Waldo Fisher, Northwestern's assistant athletic director, who had said of Paddy:

"He started it all."

What Waldo meant is that the university's sports tradition; the fighting spirit of its teams, and the "N" Men's club itself began with the 145 pound Irishman, who may have

[CHICAGO'S AMERICAN photo by Tony Berardi Jr.]

PADDY DRISCOLL [2d from left] receives awards from Stu Holcomb, Northwestern's athletic director [left], and Robert Mackey, president of "N" Men's club. Northwestern football Coach Alex Agase looks on.

been the greatest football player ever.

Four of the men who had played with Paddy on the teams of 1915-'16 were there to take a bow with their quarterback and captain. Dutch Rose, John Thomas, Bligh Grassett and Carroll [Bill] Johnson came out to be with Paddy again as did stars of later eras such as Don Clawson, Pug Rentner, Henry Penfield, Don Heap, Bill DeCorrevont, Don Stonesifer and Steve Sawle.

AFTER HE had received the "N" Men's award for "legendary achievements," Paddy got up to say, "You don't get these things every day you know," and he was off.

When Paddy's talk had ended, a husky ex-football player described the speech as "cute." He wasn't using the word in its modern, cynical connotation. He meant that Paddy was warm and gentle and genuine.

In his 69th year and full of honors, Driscoll neither understands nor believes in his greatness. His little anecdotes always poke fun at Driscoll, the football player, a performer who never was funny to the opposition.

All the stories had been heard before, because they are part of the legend, but Paddy added wry observations that changed the perspective.

EVERYBODY IN THE hall knew that Paddy had drop kicked a field goal from 55 yards out at Hammond without knowing what he had wrought because he had been rapped on the head on the previous play. Last night he offered this commentary on history:

"I must have been insane to try to kick it that far."

He told of playing in a pro grame against Jim Thorpe.

"I liked to run back those kickoffs," he said, "because you could dodge around, but this day I didn't zig when I should have and that Thorpe and Doc Spears got me in a vise.

"I had never stopped so fast in my life, and I haven't since."

And just before he sat down, Paddy told the capacity crowd:

"Thanks for throwing me the party."

PADDY IS TO BE enshrined next month in the Pro Football Hall of Fame in Canton, O., but he had yet to be nominated for the collegiate Hall of Fame. Members of the "N" club are seeing purple over college football's slight of their man and rightly so.

Everybody ... whereas ... Fo ...

Gale Sayers signed this football as the 1965 NFL Rookie of the Year.

Gale Sayers
Roy 65
1965 Rookie of the Year

1972 SPORTS FOCUS FOOTBALL ISSUE
Chicago Bears

$1.50

The 1972 Bears yearbook featured Dick Butkus on its cover.

BUTKUS
51

Dick Butkus HOF 79

THE BEARS' MONDAY NIGHT DEBUT

The National Football League turned on the lights when ABC's *Monday Night Football* signed on from Cleveland Municipal Stadium at 8 PM CST on September 21, 1970. In that contest, unlike any prior televised football game, impresario Roone Arledge created a bombastic three-man announcing team: Keith Jackson on the play-by-play, quirky ex-Dallas quarterback Don Meredith, and the brash, attention-grabbing Howard Cosell. They described a wild and woolly Browns victory, 31–21, over Joe Namath's New York Jets. Advertisers paid $65,000 per minute that night. And when the telecast drew 33 percent of the viewing audience, the people who paid

ABC's Monday Night Football *crew included (from left) Howard Cosell, Frank Gifford, and "Dandy" Don Meredith. They called the action from 1971 through 1984. Overall, the Bears are 19–33 since the series began in 1970.*

NOT SO HOT: THE BEARS ON MONDAY NIGHT

The Bears have had many memorable Monday night moments but far more on the losing side. In 52 Monday nighters, the Bears have won 19 games and lost 33. At home in Soldier Field, they are 11–11 compared to a disastrous 8–22 on the road.

The nights to remember came in the Mike Ditka era from 1982 to 1992. During that time, Iron Mike's teams went 8–12. In a 38–24 loss to Miami on December 2, 1985, the Bears and Dolphins played for a record Monday night audience: a 29.6 Nielsen rating and 46.0 share.

the bills knew they'd struck a bargain-basement deal. They watched the franchise grow.

Two weeks later, the league had a dream matchup between ancient "black and blue" rivals, the Bears and the Detroit Lions. To maximize the large Chicago audience, the game was played at Detroit's Tiger Stadium. On October 5, Cosell's perfect, nasal voice extolled the virtues of "George Halas's Monsters of the Midway led by Dick *Butkus*!"

Jim Dooley's fired-up Bears roared out to a 7–0 lead on a 20-yard Jack Concannon to Dick Gordon scoring pass. The lead held up until the third quarter when the methodical Lions ground out three touchdowns to get ahead 21–7. Before Cosell and Meredith could break out the gabby "blowout package" broadcasters use to pad a going-nowhere game, the Bears gained new life when Concannon teamed up with Gordon on a fourth-quarter, 60-yard touchdown pass.

But they got no closer as Dick LeBeau intercepted Concannon and ran it back to the Bears' 33, after which Mel Farr scored his second touchdown to ice a 28–14 Detroit victory. It turned out the lights in that game, but the party was just beginning for *MNF.*

1971: SOLDIER FIELD IS HOME

By the late '60s, the Bears knew their days at Wrigley Field were numbered; commissioner Pete Rozelle decreed that all NFL arenas must have a *minimum* of 50,000 seats. Comiskey Park on the South Side was not an option. After an early-season 20–16 win over the Eagles at Northwestern's Dyche Stadium in 1970, nearby Evanston residents railed at the drunken behavior of celebrating fans, and the Evanston City Council banned the Bears from returning.

With nowhere to play, George Halas had to go to the Chicago Park District for a long-term lease on Soldier Field. Built as a World War I memorial in 1924, its plumbing dated back that far, and 110,000 of its seats were some of the worst in any stadium. The place was a monstrosity.

They filled it a couple of times, when 111,000 attended the 1926 Army-Navy game. And the Gene Tunney–Jack Dempsey heavyweight title fight in 1927 was the celebrated event of the Roaring '20s. But the largest crowd of all came in 1937, when 115,000 fans squeezed in to see phenom Bill DeCorrevont

Built in 1924 as Grant Park Municipal Stadium and dedicated as Soldier Field in 1925, the stadium was rarely used until the Bears moved there in 1971; the biggest crowd Soldier Field saw before the Bears was an audience of 115,000 for the 1937 city championship high school game between Leo and Austin.

Rick Casares finishes a 28-yard touchdown run as the visiting Bears rout the Cardinals 31–7 in the finale of their bitter crosstown rivalry on November 29, 1959, at Soldier Field. The Cardinals relocated to St. Louis in 1960 and moved again to Arizona in 1988.

and Austin beat Leo for the city high school title. Otherwise, except for the annual College All-Star football game, the Bears' annual Armed Forces game that ended the preseason, and high school playoffs, Soldier Field was a seldom-used white elephant on the lakefront.

However, there were pros to the millions the Bears had to pay in rent. In 1959, the Park District had moved the playing field to the south bowl and replaced the auto-racing track with field box seats. An artificial surface was installed before the Bears arrived in 1971. The Bears also brought Ralph Brizzolara's bleachers from Wrigley Field and had them erected near the north end zone for a new capacity of 57,000.

The place fell down around fans until the Bears and the Park District agreed to build a modern stadium on the Soldier Field site. The Bears played in Champaign, Illinois, in 2002 while construction crews built the new facility. It's a 61,000-seat arena with superior sightlines inside the old colonnades. But most of all, it is Chicago, and it is home.

ABE

"What a way to go!" Abe Gibron's Chicago-area Ford commercials were hilarious. Gibron, dressed in a neon-orange ballcap, a matching coach's shirt, and navy blue polyester slacks—coupled with actress Melody Rogers—was the best show in town from 1972 through 1974.

Gibron's Chicago Bears weren't that good at football. But there was never a dull moment around the team, whether at Soldier Field where the Bears practiced or in the cramped chaos of the team offices at 173 West Madison Street, above the "L" on the Wells Street side of Chicago's Loop.

Ironically, Abe was a terrific assistant and motivator— almost as good as he was as a professional football lineman. A Purdue alum, Abe came to the NFL with the Cleveland Browns in 1950 as a 5′11″ guard who played at 243 pounds— and he got bigger and bigger as the years passed. Smart, fast, and quick for his size, the tough Gibron was a favorite of Paul Brown in Cleveland's championship run when the Browns won three NFL titles and three division titles through 1955.

Brown cut him in 1957, and in 1958, with his career floundering in Philadelphia, Gibron was given a chance by George Halas. A grateful Gibron responded with two brilliant seasons, anchoring a Bears line that could whip everybody but the world champion Baltimore Colts. He began coaching with the Bears in 1960 and would remain a part of the team for the next 15 seasons as an assistant and then as head coach.

No coach ever had a more loyal press following. Commuting from his lifelong hometown, Michigan City, Indiana, Gibron, first and foremost, was a party animal. His cookouts were legendary: roast lambs on a spit, side dishes galore, and tubs of iced beer everywhere on the spacious lawn. He and his wife, Susie, entertained like royalty.

But Gibron as a head coach just wasn't that interested in the fine points of football that he learned in Paul Brown's classroom or on George Halas's staff, which had been filled with superb assistants and technicians such as George Allen, Chuck Mather, and Jim Dooley. "Just give me my little gang of street fighters," Abe would say. "We may or may not win, but you'll know you were in a battle. For sure."

Finally, the Gibron record, 11–30–1, told the final score. Abe went off to Tampa Bay to join old pal John McKay, coach for the Buccaneers. He died there on September 23, 1997, a day after his 72nd birthday.

Abe Gibron finished his playing career with the Bears in 1959; he became an assistant in 1960 and was a head coach from 1972 to 1974. He was beloved by George Halas and a Chicago favorite.

JIM FINKS: THE CHANGE MAKER

Jim Finks was a football lifer, starting from his coal-country upbringing in downstate Salem, Illinois, through the gritty postwar NFL as the first T formation quarterback for the Pittsburgh Steelers, to several years with the Canadian Football League, and finally as the master builder of the Minnesota Vikings.

George Halas Jr., or "Mugs" as he was known in the locker room, convinced his father that change was mandatory. On September 12, 1974, Mugs hired Finks as general manager and executive vice president and gave him unprecedented total control. Finks's plans were bigger than any one man, and he made them work. He retooled everything, remaking the Bears into a model organization. He changed the chartered airline, spruced up the uniform, and switched broadcast outlets and announcers. He even moved the club offices to Chicago's high-rent district at 55 East Jackson. Meanwhile, he conceived and executed a plan to establish the entire operation in a modern facility he named Halas Hall, on the campus of north suburban Lake Forest College.

He hired new coaches, added competent scouts, and drafted wisely—the first player he chose was Jackson State running back Walter Payton. Next, he assembled capable linemen on both the offensive and defensive sides of the ball. He even invited the media to watch and report on the progress of the team as it developed, which

A Hall of Fame executive, Jim Finks arrived in 1974, rebuilt the Bears, drafted the Super Bowl players, and left in 1983 after a job well done.

LAKE FOREST: ALL DAY, EVERY DAY

George Halas first took the Bears to training camp among the cornfields of St. Joseph's College in Rensselaer, Indiana, in 1944. The players were hit with two practices a day and were forced—hot, panting, and parched—to run the torturous Halas Mile. However, they also bonded and prepared themselves for championship seasons.

Jim Finks wanted everything in a single place. So, in 1975, he moved the football side of the operation, from training camp to regular-season practice, to Lake Forest College in the affluent north suburb. Finks made that address an NFL dateline when George Halas Sr. dedicated Halas Hall in the name of his son in 1979. The Bears trained there in summers until 1984, when they moved to Platteville, Wisconsin.

would have been unheard of with Halas at the controls.

Well aware that long-time NFL linebacker Jack Pardee had coached his 1974 World Football League team to its championship game, Finks figured he was the right man for the tough job of head coach. In 1977, Pardee's Bears closed with a six-game winning streak. They made the playoffs on Bob Thomas's field goal at the end of

Cornerback Virgil Livers and linebacker Bob Pifferini were two players from Jack Pardee's coaching years (1975–1977). They were a part of Jim Finks's rebuilt Bears.

overtime in the ice and snow of Giants Stadium, beating New York 12–9. Regardless, three weeks after a playoff loss in Dallas, Pardee fled to Washington and Finks had to land a new coach: Minnesota defensive coordinator Neill Armstrong.

HERE COME THE HONEY BEARS!

When octogenarian George Halas saw the Dallas Cowboys cheerleaders cavort on television in 1976, the old impresario was hooked. He called general manager Jim Finks in the morning. "Kid," Halas said, "if those oil-rich rubes from Dallas can stage a show like that, so can we!"

As author Roy Taylor wrote in *Chicago Bears History,* Cathy Core, a professional choreographer, had just moved to Chicago from New Jersey. A parishioner in Core's new church was a friend of Finks and was well aware of Finks's marching orders. He called Finks and told him he might have the answer—he should call Core.

Core actually hung up on the caller who identified himself as the general manager of the Chicago Bears—she thought it was a crank call. Finks finally reached her through their mutual friend and invited her for an interview at 55 East Jackson. Finks hired her on the spot and took her to meet George Halas himself. "As long as I'm alive," Papa Bear said, "we will have dancing girls on the sidelines!"

In short order, Core visited Dallas and then Denver to interview those clubs about their cheerleading squads; she sifted through scores of applications, conducted interviews, held tryouts, and whittled the list down to 20 women. That fall, she introduced them as the Honey Bears.

And what a sight they were. Bear fans will always remember the chorus line of striking and smiling young women—the taller the better—with teased hair, uniformed in white vests over orange long-sleeved blouses, short white shorts, and high white boots, and waving orange and blue pompons. They earned every penny of their $15-per-game salary.

After Halas died in 1983, the McCaskeys tried to put an end to the Honey Bears, but Core produced a contract that was valid through 1985. Thus, the Honey Bears remained through Super Bowl XX—that singular shining season in Chicago Bears history—making friends and new fans wherever they went.

After the Super Bowl, Virginia Halas McCaskey, who thought that the ladies her father loved and doted on looked cheap, made an executive decision. She ordered her son, Michael, to tell general manager Jerry Vainisi to cancel the act. However, as a McCaskey son related years later, when Virginia McCaskey is no longer in charge, the Honey Bears will return. And everyone will delight, especially the spirit of George Halas.

> **"AS LONG AS I'M ALIVE," PAPA BEAR SAID, "WE WILL HAVE DANCING GIRLS ON THE SIDELINES!"**

The Honey Bears pose in all their energetic and crowd-pleasing glory. Everybody loved them except for Virginia McCaskey, who got rid of them after the 1985 Super Bowl season. Is there a curse?

THE AMAZING WALTER PAYTON

Jim Finks made the easiest draft-day decision of his life in 1975 when he called the name of Walter Payton from Jackson State. Payton could bench press 300 pounds and walk the length of a football field *on his hands.* Finks managed to land a franchise player who Mike Ditka has called the best-ever running back in the National Football League.

The Atlanta Falcons opened the draft by taking Cal quarterback Steve Bartkowski. The Dallas Cowboys then chose Randy White, a future Hall of Fame defensive tackle from Maryland. The Baltimore Colts jumped at the chance to take

1977: A 14-YEAR PLAYOFF DROUGHT ENDS

The Bears were trailing Kansas City 27–21 at Soldier Field on November 5, 1977. With time running out, Bob Avellini fired long to a wide-open Greg Latta in the south end zone, gaining an impossible 28–27 victory. That ignited a five-game winning streak heading into a New York finale.

When an ice storm made footing impossible, *Chicago Tribune* columnist Bob Markus found a sporting goods operator to bring the shoes that saved Chicago. It was 9–9, late in overtime, when the Bears lined up for a field goal. Avellini held for Bob Thomas, and the future Illinois Supreme Court Chief Justice delivered the 12–9 winner. The Bears lost 37–7 in Dallas a week later, but their first playoff season since 1963 was a success.

now-forgotten offensive guard Ken Huff of North Carolina. Somehow, Walter Jerry Payton, the best player in any draft, lasted until the fourth selection.

Payton was just 21 years old when the 1975 season started. He gained no yards on eight carries in an opening day loss, 35–7, to the Colts. Then he got moving. By season's end he had gained 679 yards—the future was promising. By 1976, when he gained 1,390 yards to lead the NFC, he was considered the best player in the league. That was a mere prelude to what came in 1977.

Payton was running away with the league rushing title by October 30 when the Bears rolled into Green Bay. He led a 26–0 victory by rushing for 205 yards, tying Gale Sayers's 1968 team mark, which was also set against the Packers. Then on November 20, on an unseasonably warm day in steady rain, Payton gained a league-record 275 yards on 40 carries in a 10–7 win over the Minnesota Vikings. He finished the season with 1,852 yards to lead the league in rushing for the only time in his 13-year career. They called him Sweetness, but Walter Payton really should have been called Greatness.

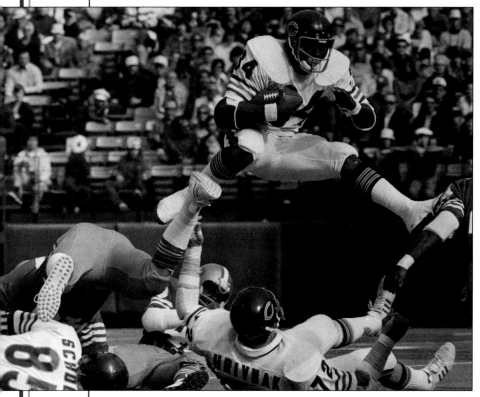

With blocks from Steve Schubert (85) and Gerry Hrivnak (72), rookie Walter Payton (34) gives a preview of things to come as he goes airborne against the San Francisco 49ers in a 31–3 Bears loss on November 16, 1975, at Candlestick Park.

Brian Piccolo's first name was misspelled on this trading card!

Bryon PICCOLO
CHICAGO BEARS • RUNNING BACK

Mike Ditka played in 84 straight games with the Bears, wearing his number 89 jersey.

George Halas poses with his 1958 coaching staff, (left to right) Chuck Mather, Paddy Driscoll, Halas, Phil Handler, Clark Shaughnessy, and Luke Johnsos.

Stan Jones played as an offensive and defensive lineman for the Bears. He was elected to the Pro Football Hall of Fame in 1991, when this photo was signed.

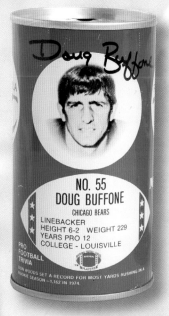

Both Doug Buffone and Johnny Musso are honored on these RC Cola cans.

The white "C" on this replica helmet is the Bears' original logo.

Old Style salutes Dick Butkus as one of Chicago's all-time greatest athletes.

STARS OF THE ERA

The years from 1964 to 1981 are, for the most part, a black hole in Bears history. Just one veteran of note was on board when Jim Finks arrived in 1974 to rebuild the program from scratch. That was outside linebacker **Doug Buffone,** the final player chosen by George Allen and the last man to have played for George Halas when he was head coach. Buffone was no All-Pro, but he was a solid performer who understood how to play like a professional. He retired in 1979 as one of the last true elder statesmen of the league.

The most colorful, controversial player of that time was left-handed quarterback **Bobby Douglass,** who had a shotgun for an arm with shotgun results: passes landing everywhere but right on target. Fans and sportswriters wanted Douglass—who was big, strong, and a force to be reckoned with in the open field—to play tight end. But Halas, the ultimate boss, stood by the erratic blond bomber. Douglass was a terrific runner, gaining 968 yards on the ground in 1972—a league record for a quarterback that stood for more than 30 years. Passing, though, was another matter. In that same '72 season, he put up only 1,246 yards through the air with nine touchdown passes against 12 interceptions and a puny 49.8 passer rating. Finks cut Douglass in 1975 after a season-opening 35–7 loss to the Colts.

Finks dug deep in the draft to find two standout safeties. Hard-hitting—some would say

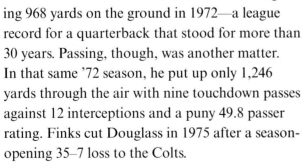

Doug Buffone

bordering on suicidal—**Doug Plank** arrived in Round 12 from Ohio State in 1975. Plank, a quick defender and sure tackler who wore number 46, became the inspiration for Buddy Ryan's famed "46 defense" that terrorized the league long after Plank retired. Barrington, Illinois, native and Yale graduate **Gary Fencik,** a superb pass defender and outstanding tackler, arrived a year later as a waiver pickup from the Miami Dolphins to become an All-Pro and 12-year mainstay through 1987. No other player in Bears history has recorded more takeaways than Fencik's 50; he intercepted 38 passes and recovered 12 fumbles. During their time together, Plank and Fencik were known around the league as "The Hit Men."

Beginning in 1979, Finks really hit it big in the first round of the draft. It all started when he landed perhaps the NFL's greatest defensive lineman of the '80s: future Hall of Famer **Dan Hampton** from Arkansas. Everybody loved *The Super Bowl Shuffle* when it first aired, but the blue-collar Hampton thought it was too cocky, and so he turned down the invitation to be featured in the music video. Finks later added linebacker **Al Harris** from Arizona State in '79. Harris excelled as both an end and a linebacker, although he missed out on the Super Bowl season of 1985 because of a contract dispute.

Dan Hampton

Gary Fencik

NEILL ARMSTRONG: THE QUIET MAN

When Jack Pardee jilted the Bears in early 1978 for the Washington Redskins, Jim Finks initially turned to the brilliant offensive mind of Bill Walsh, who had just finished his first year as Stanford's head coach. But Walsh wanted something Finks would never surrender: personnel say-so and his own team. Aware that his opportunity would soon come with the troubled San Francisco 49ers, Walsh politely said no.

Finks, who always operated with plenty of options, turned to a trusted ally from his time in Minnesota: the Vikings' quiet but effective defensive coordinator, Neill Armstrong. Armstrong was a superb end at Oklahoma A&M, the top draft choice for Philadelphia in 1947, and a key contributor to the Eagles' championship teams of 1948 and '49. In 1951, he jumped to the Winnipeg Blue Bombers of the Canadian Football League, where he played until 1954 with former Eagle teammate Bud Grant. Grant was then named

Neill Armstrong was the Bears head coach from 1978 to 1981. He was a true gentleman who was too "nice" for George Halas's liking. He was replaced by Mike Ditka in 1982.

the Bombers' head coach, and he remained there for ten years. Armstrong was coaching at Edmonton when he joined Finks and Grant in 1970 as Minnesota's defensive coordinator.

When Armstrong faltered in 1978 with the core of Pardee's playoff team, Finks's confidence never wavered. It certainly helped when Armstrong's Bears beat Pardee and the Redskins 14–10 at RFK Stadium, salvaging a disappointing 7–9 season. And Finks's faith was finally vindicated in 1979, when quarterback Mike Phipps led the Bears to a 7–1 finish.

Before the season finale at Soldier Field, to make the playoffs the Bears—to borrow a poker term—had to draw an inside straight due to the NFL's tie-breaking system: They had to beat St. Louis and hope Dallas defeated Washington, with the difference in points scored and allowed between the two games favoring the Bears by 34 points.

But as the players arrived, they were greeted by a crushing loss: Team president Mugs Halas had died from a massive heart attack during the night. Armstrong shared the unfortunate news with his club in the locker room and used the tragedy as extra motivation. The Bears did their part and then some, as they routed the Cardinals 42–6. In turn, Roger Staubach led the Cowboys to a victory over their rival Redskins, which unexpectedly sent the Bears to the playoffs as a wild-card entry—they would face the Eagles.

Victory over Philadelphia in the postseason seemed all but a foregone conclusion when Walter Payton ran 84 yards for a touchdown in the early going, but a late flag for illegal motion killed the play. The Bears went on to lose 27–17. The quiet, kind, and gentle Armstrong, a players' coach if there ever was one, never had control of that team again. A 7–9 campaign in 1980 and then a 6–10 collapse in '81 sealed his doom. Halas, back in charge after Mugs's death, dropped the other shoe at season's end. He had a game plan, and neither Finks nor Armstrong figured into it.

A DEATH IN THE HALAS FAMILY CHANGES EVERYTHING

Life had never been better for George Stanley "Mugs" Halas than it was on Saturday night, December 15, 1979. His 84-year-old father, George Sr., had recently granted him counsel and bestowed approval on controller Jerry Vainisi for an estate plan that would assure an orderly and cost-saving transition in the event of his death.

It was understood from the beginning, when he was born in 1925, that Mugs was the designated heir to the football team. Period. Papa Bear would take proper financial care of daughter Virginia and her 11 McCaskey children, but they would play no role whatsoever in the operation of the football team.

Mugs Halas had two children, Stephen and Christine, by his first wife, Terry. Once the smoke had cleared from a bitter divorce, Mugs remarried in 1978. He and his wife, Pat, lived in a Water Tower Place condo in downtown Chicago. Mugs had given Jim Finks total control of the

George "Mugs" Halas Jr. works at his desk in the Bears offices at 55 E. Jackson in Chicago. The designated heir to George Halas Sr., Mugs was the team president when he died at age 53 on December 16, 1979, from a massive heart attack. His sister, Virginia McCaskey, became heiress.

team and was pleased with the direction things were moving. The Bears had made the playoffs in 1977 and had another chance the next day if a very complicated and unlikely set of circumstances occured. The Bears would need to beat the St. Louis Cardinals, the Dallas Cowboys would need to beat the Washington Redskins, and the difference in points scored and allowed between the two games would need to be at least 34 points in the Bears' favor.

Sometime in the early hours of Sunday morning, December 16, 1979, Mugs was stricken with a massive coronary. He was dead by the time the emergency medics arrived at the apartment. Virginia McCaskey's husband, Ed, immediately dispatched the favored grandson, Tim, to George Halas's building to inform him before anyone else could break the word. The death occured too late to make the Sunday papers, and the family was able to keep the news off the radio and television until 8 AM.

Driving through rain and sleet, Tim arrived within seconds of Halas's physician and saw his grandfather weeping. The entire NFL hierarchy, led by Commissioner Pete Rozelle, came to Chicago for the wake and funeral on December 19.

Halas Sr. went into seclusion for the next eight months. He refused to see or talk to anyone outside the family except the trusted Vainisi, to whom he issued an order—under no circumstances was anyone to set foot in Mugs's office or disturb anything on his desk. Nobody else was allowed to make any operational decisions. Vainisi had to redraw the estate with attorneys from Kirkland and Ellis.

When he came back to the office during mid-summer 1980, Halas, by then 85 years old, issued the following edict, "Only a Halas can be team president." That meant the founder was back in charge—nobody had any idea what he had in mind.

GAME DAY: END OF THE HALAS ERA

By 1980, the founder of the Chicago Bears, George Halas, was an elder statesman-in-residence. He was the team patriarch and an active godfather figure to the league. He had again become a vital presence as the team's president and majordomo, the way he had been before he put matters in Mugs's hands.

Trying to rebuild a football team was a slow process, which was not surprising in such an unwieldy league. The glamour teams that drew the fans, as well as media interest, and made game-changing innovations—the kind of innovations that had belonged to Halas and the Bears in the past—included two teams that were founded in 1960: the Dallas Cowboys of the NFL and the Oakland Raiders of the AFL. The Pittsburgh Steelers, a third old-line team that was now a part of the AFC, had built a dynasty to rival those of the Bears, Browns, and Packers of old.

Quarterback Jim McMahon (9) takes the snap and rolls out with running back Walter Payton (34) in a 1980s game against the Lions.

1980 MILESTONES

For two weeks in late 1980, the Bears were the talk of the league. It began on November 27, at the Pontiac Silverdome against the Detroit Lions. After quarterback Vince Evans scored to send the game into overtime, reserve back David Williams took Eddie Murray's kickoff at his 5-yard line, shot upfield, cut to the outside, and went untouched for 95 yards. The play took 21 seconds—the shortest overtime ever.

The following week, in the warm rain of Soldier Field, the Bears socked it to the Green Bay Packers 61–7. Evans went 18 for 22 with 316 yards and three touchdowns. Walter Payton added three more touchdowns on the ground. After the game, Coach Neill Armstrong said that he did not run up the score: "I never gloat. It just happened."

The Bears of the early '80s were not much to get worked up about. They couldn't put together a consistent offense, they didn't have a consistent a quarterback, nor could they sustain any level of competence despite the presence of the best player in the league: Walter Payton. But Jim Finks had been drafting well and had assembled parts that might be ready for a run. However, the team's success was contingent on finding the right coach to lead them. When Halas decided that the next field general would have to be a real Bear—a Bear in his image—interest began to swirl about the club once again.

Halas settled on one-time bad-boy tight end Mike Ditka, who he had exiled into NFL purgatory in Philadelphia for publicly defying him. The talk suddenly took on real meaning, and for the first time in far too long, the Chicago Bears were about to become a dominant NFL presence once again.

Gale Sayers's 1966 card (left) was issued after his rookie season. The other is from 1970.

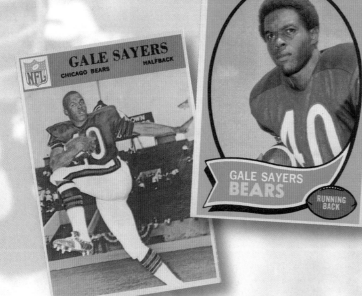

The Midwest Shrine Game is a yearly Packers event. It began in 1950 and continues today. In 1966, in the 17th annual contest, Chicago won 13-10. But the Packers came back in 1967 to beat the Bears 18-0.

Dick Butkus was just a rookie on this 1965 trading card.

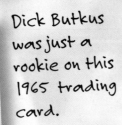

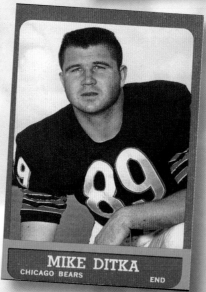

This 1965 Mike Ditka trading card came out a year before his Bears playing career ended.

Walter Payton borrowed these thigh pads from a friend in high school. After Payton started college, the friend wanted them back, but Payton said he was still using them. After being in the NFL for a couple years, Payton saw the old friend, who asked about the thigh pads. Payton was still wearing them.

The back of Walter Payton's rookie card shows that he led the team with 679 rushing yards. In 1976, he became a star, gaining 1,390 yards—second in the league.

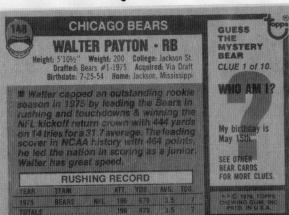

CHICAGO BEARS

WALTER PAYTON · RB

Height: 5'10½" Weight: 200 College: Jackson St.
Drafted: Bears #1-1975 Acquired: Via Draft
Birthdate: 7-25-54 Home: Jackson, Mississippi

Walter capped an outstanding rookie season in 1975 by leading the Bears in rushing and touchdowns and winning the NFL kickoff return crown with 444 yards on 14 tries for a 31.7 average. The leading scorer in NCAA history with 464 points, he led the nation in scoring as a junior. Walter has great speed.

GUESS THE MYSTERY BEAR
CLUE 1 of 10.

WHO AM I?

My birthday is May 15th.

SEE OTHER BEAR CARDS FOR MORE CLUES.

RUSHING RECORD

YEAR	TEAM		ATT.	YDS.	AVG.	TDS.
1975	BEARS	NFL	196	679	3.5	7
TOTALS			196	679	3.5	7

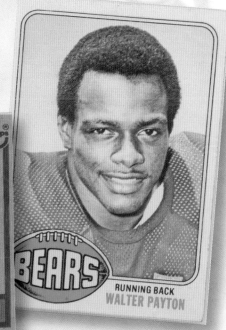

RUNNING BACK
WALTER PAYTON

Walter Payton was the NFL kick returns leader in 1975, his rookie year, which earned him this trophy. It has been said that he used it as a doorstop.

WALTER PAYTON
CHICAGO BEARS
1975 NFC Kick-Off Returns Champion
31.7 Yards Per Return

National Football League Players Association

On October 31, 1977, the *Chicago Tribune* featured Walter Payton's 205-yard rushing game. He led the Bears to a 27–0 rout over the Packers at Lambeau Field.

Chicago Tribune
Monday, October 31, 1977

Sports/Business

Section 6

Payton, Bears frolic over Green Bay

Walter ties team record of 205 yards

By Don Pierson
Chicago Tribune Press Service

GREEN BAY, Wis.—Ballet's loss is football's gain. Walter Payton could have been another Rudolf Nureyev, who never has to share the glory with his other performers.

But this is an 11-man sport, played in dirt and sweat that often obscures its beauty. Sunday afternoon, Payton turned Lambeau Field into a stage and danced for 205 yards in front of 56,267 fans who thought they had paid to see

Two teams block, tackle, pass, score points, and do other mundane things.

The scoreboard read Bears 20, Packers 0, but that wasn't what people watched. They had become mesmerized by a man who should have been wearing leotards and slippers rather than shoulder pads and cleats.

And when he was done jumping over fallen bodies, pirouetting away from tacklers, forecasting linebackers, dragging bodies across the goal line, and helping his victims to their feet, he said: "Anybody couldn't do it."

PAYTON ALWAYS SAYS that. Against the Packers, he may be right. Johnny Musso gained 61 yards. Robin Earl gained 44. Bob Avellini ran four times for 36, matching the four games he completed for offensive air. But he didn't have to throw in the second half.

"It was an easy game to call," Avellini said after sneaking 34 yards for a touchdown in the fourth quarter and hitting Mike Phipps finish.

It was the first shutout for the Bears since 1972, when they beat Cleveland 17-0 in Abe Gibron's first National Football League coaching victory.

Payton ran 23 times and scored two touchdowns before leaving with 10:35 to play, deadlocking another virtuoso of another era, Gale Sayers.

It was in this field Nov. 3, 1968, that Sayers entered the Bears' record book with 205 yards. Payton didn't get a chance to break that record, but said he didn't care. He can take some satisfaction in knowing it took Sayers 24 carries.

PAYTON HAD TO talk his way into 205.

"We weren't going to send him in on that final series," said Coach Jack Pardee, "but he wanted a personal goal of 200."

Payton carried for eight yards and then trotted off. The press box called the bench to inform Payton that Payton he wanted to return. "He talked me into it," said Sayers' team record.

Pardee said Payton "mentioned" that he wanted to return. "He talked me into it once, but he said twice," Pardee said. "He wasn't adamant after three. Walter will be more important to us next week."

"I didn't want to break Sayers' record because Sayers is a super guy," Payton said. "What's a record? I just wanted to win the game. I didn't want to figure out all the attention. I wanted to see him break the re-

Continued on page 3, col. 1

For Packers, it was a day for broken tackles, boos

GREEN BAY, Wis.—Yes, Walter Payton almost was unbelievable Sunday. Unbelievable, unreal, and unrelenting in putting the Bears to a 26-0 victory over the Packers.

"Payton just breaks those tackles when you think you have him nailed," shrugged Bob Bacher, Green Bay's defensive end. "You think you have both arms wrapped around Payton and still he gets away. He's a great runner."

"Payton has such quickness, such acceleration, and for certainly is tough. He's so tough that you can hit him head-on and he'll get up to grab a few more yards," said Jim Carter, Packer linebacker. "Payton is no superman, but we may have put him in the Hall of Fame the way we let him break loose."

At times, the elusive Bear runner seemed more like a Halloween ghost as floating free from the Packers' clutches. Rushing for 205 yards, or possibly a record 266 after the statistics are reviewed, the mercurial Chicagoan left the Packers little more than handfuls of his afternoon's cutery air. Or, as the Packers overwhelmed, "He breaks our tackles."

David Condon

Wake of the News

fights for yardage. Payton will gore you, and you very seldom get a high shot at him because he ducks down when he's about to be stopped. He ducks down and digs out those extra inches."

"We just did too much grabbing and reaching for Payton and not enough of getting a solid hold on him," Carter

The truth is that the Bears completely ran the ball down our throats. They played like most people know the Bears can play.

Packer Coach Bart Starr

BART STARR, the Packer coach who was "embarrassed" by the one-sided story of Chicago's triumph, said: "I want to preface my comments by noting that I'd hate to say something that could be construed as diminishing Payton's great afternoon.

"But many times when you see such yardage totals, it's because there's been a lot of missed tackles. I won't know until I see the films, but we did see indications that we missed tackling opportunities. Of course, Payton is an objective target.

"The truth is that the Bears completely ran the ball down our throats. They played like most people know the Bears can play. Bob Avellini's passing game complimented Payton's running.

"Yes, this has to be our worst defeat the Packers have had in 1977, because we've been close in all the other contests. Against the Bears, we weren't remotely in the ball game."

PAYTON'S contribution of 205 yards rushing equals the Bear record that Gale Sayers set in Packertown in 1968. However, there's a chance that Payton may have surpassed Sayers' record. The unofficial statistics show him with 205 yards gained, and it will be up to league office to determine Payton's official yardage.

Starr was the quarterback on Sayers' afternoon, but doesn't remember it particularly.

"Every time I played against Sayers he ran for lots of yards," said Starr. "The Bears deserve credit for housing back after not playing well in some earlier games."

Starr sighed, shrugged, and left. It was obvious that although the Packer coach may have forgotten details of Sayers' great afternoon, he'll long be haunted by memories of Payton's phantomlike running.

PACKER LINEBACKER Fred Carr said succinctly: "We were hurt by Payton, but missing the tackles. If we could have held on to him, it would have been a different story."

Barber added: "It may look like Payton is giving you a leg and then jerking it away, but he's just a good runner. He

LYNN DICKEY, THE PACKERS' harassed quarterback, saw Payton's great performance from another viewpoint, saying:

"Defensively, the Bears didn't do anything we didn't anticipate. We'd see something started and then sputter. Everything turned bad; when it rains it pours.

"Sure the defense pressured me, but attribute that to Payton. With a guy like Payton gearing the offense, their defense can turn it all loose.

"We prepared for them, but Payton put them on top and that got their defense on edge," when you're on top you can do almost anything you want. They seemed to blitz more than usual or threatened more often."

As the PACKERS' builders afternoon wore on, home fans began booing. Dickey said: "Yeah, I heard 'em early, when things go bad, the quarterback is the first to get it. That's the bad part about playing the position; it leaves you no place to hide."

"I've heard booing before," Carter said. "I've been around a long time."

"The boos? You've there right I heard them," Starr said. "I hope they were directed at us (Almost directed at at the team."

Boos for the Packers, cheers for Payton. This was Sunday evening that a check of the official play-by-play showed that Payton might have gained one more yard than he was credited. Payton's play-by-play totals give Payton's first-

Continued on page 3, col. 4

Although an unidentified Green Bay Packer had his hands on the Bears' Walter Payton, he couldn't bring him down. Sunday, it was a familiar situation for the Packers. Payton carried the ball 23 times for 205 yards.

Hawks count fans while

Inside:
At least somebody in Buffalo

CHAPTER FOUR

THE AGE OF IRON MIKE

1982–1992

"It is a situation that was meant for me.

Everybody has their destiny, and mine is Chicago."

MIKE DITKA, JANUARY 21, 1982

Above: *In* Da Coach, *by Rich Wolfe, Mike Ditka's friends, drinking buddies, ex-players, and team-mates spin yarns about the coach and Hall of Fame tight end.* **Right:** *Walter Payton is on his way to a long gain against the Green Bay Packers on October 30, 1977, at Lambeau Field.*

IRON MIKE

George Halas's courtship of Mike Ditka could not begin in earnest until the Dallas Cowboys were knocked out of the 1981–82 playoffs, although rumors had been flying like shrapnel in a war zone since November 1981. According to Ditka in *Papa Bear: The Life and Legacy of George Halas,* Halas and Sid Luckman were watching the Thanksgiving telecast of the Bears and Dallas Cowboys at Halas's apartment when he said, "He's our next coach!" Halas was talking about Ditka—a player who drew his ire and a player he banished in 1967, when Ditka accused the old coach of nursing nickels like manhole covers.

By Christmas week, the drumbeat for Neill Armstrong's ouster was rolling. Without consulting Jim Finks, his general manager, Halas called a Christmas Eve news conference. "The defensive players," Halas said, "have written me a letter to retain Buddy Ryan as defensive coordinator." Two days later,

On January 20, 1982, at the team offices at 55 East Jackson, George Halas (who would turn 87 two weeks later) has just announced the hiring of his former tight end Mike Ditka. Ditka became the team's tenth head coach.

Halas, who loved Ryan's aggressive "46 defense," announced that he had once again signed him as defensive coordinator—and had given him a raise.

By then, Jerry Vainisi had prepared two files for the boss—both on Ditka. A thick one contained notes from contract negotiations as well as investigators' reports on Ditka's considerably active nightlife in the '60s. The other was a single handwritten letter from Ditka himself, who was coaching tight ends and special teams in Dallas. Ditka said the word was out around the league that Armstrong was in trouble. "If that's the case, I want to be considered for the opportunity to fulfill my dream of bringing the Bears back to the days of glory when you were the coach, and I was a player."

Ditka gained his freedom when the San Francisco 49ers knocked the Cowboys out of the playoffs January 10, 1982. They won 28–27 due to Joe Montana's late touchdown pass to Dwight Clark, known thereafter as "The Catch." It took ten days of secret meetings and discussions to wrap up the deal. "Tell me about your coaching philosophy," Halas said in the job interview.

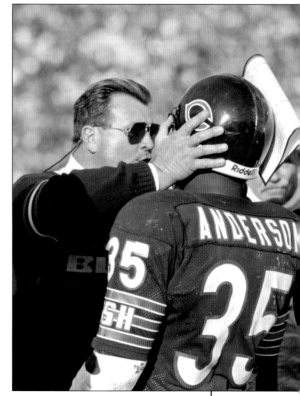

Coach Mike Ditka grabs Neal Anderson's helmet to make his point. The 1988 season saw the Bears reach their third NFC title game in the span of a decade.

Mike Ditka's first Bears team is shown here in fall 1982 at Halas Hall in Lake Forest. Many of these players were a part of the Super Bowl team. Others left after a strike-shortened season that saw the young team struggle to a 3–6 record.

"I won't B.S. you, Coach," Ditka said. "Your coaching philosophy is the same as mine. I want to win. I know how to win." Halas offered a three-year contract at $100,000 a year. Ditka would not accept until Halas built in two 15 percent raises. Halas had his man, the lowest paid coach in the league; Ditka had the job of his dreams.

First, Ditka needed a winning quarterback. He found one in his first 1982 pick, Brigham Young's record-setting Jim McMahon. The feisty, cocky McMahon got out of the limousine at Halas Hall drinking a beer, which evoked memories of Bobby Layne, the championship quarterback Halas let get away in 1949. McMahon was as smart as any player Ditka ever knew or coached, and he and Ditka bonded the same way Ditka had bonded with Halas—like fire and gasoline. But Iron Mike knew this kid could play—and lead. Unfortunately, a player's strike cut seven games out of the schedule during McMahon's first year, and the Bears finished at 3–6.

A year later, Finks opened the draft with two first-round picks. He started with Ditka's fellow Pittsburgh alum Jim

Covert, who was the left tackle every great offense must have to win a title. Finks followed with the fastest and most dangerous receiver in the draft, Willie Gault of Tennessee.

Like a pinball player hitting one grand finale after another, Finks panned Super Bowl diamonds in the rough: cornerback Mike Richardson of Arizona State; strong safety Dave Duerson and his Notre Dame teammate, guard Tom Thayer; and in Round 8, defensive end Richard Dent of Tennessee State and guard Mark Bortz of Iowa.

On August 24, the day after Finks signed holdout Gault, George Halas, who was now ill with cancer, called Jerry Vainisi at the downtown offices and asked him to stop by his apartment. When Vainisi arrived, Papa Bear told him that Finks had resigned and that Vainisi would be the new genreal manager, designated by Halas himself. When asked if he had told his daughter, Virginia, Halas replied, "I told her, 'I have my men in place. Jerry Vainisi and Mike Ditka. I know I have made the right decision.'"

Coach Mike Ditka talks tactics with Walter Payton during the Bears' hard-fought 27–19 victory over the Tampa Bay Buccaneers in Tampa Bay on October 6, 1985. The victory pushed the Bears record to 5–0.

THE BIGGEST SHAKEUP OF ALL

By the fall of 1983, George Halas had not been seen in public since midwinter. It was obvious something was wrong, but nobody at headquarters was talking—if indeed they knew anything. Only a chosen few, daughter Virginia McCaskey and son-in-law Ed, Jerry Vainisi, Ditka, Sid Luckman, and close friend Mike Notaro, were aware that Papa Bear was fighting a losing battle with pancreatic cancer.

That is why it was imperative for Halas to establish a management team—Vainisi and Ditka—to succeed him and run the franchise. When daughter Virginia twice tried to bring Michael, her oldest son and a Harvard Business School professor, into the operation, Halas would not allow it.

Vainisi visited Halas frequently, and he and Ditka stopped at the Edgewater Beach Apartments to see him a few days

Below: *Virginia Halas McCaskey poses with her oldest son, Michael, the grandson of team founder George Halas, before a game at Soldier Field. She reluctantly had to fire him as team president in January 1999, after a series of management missteps on his part.* Right: *The* Sun-Times*'s special section on Halas ran November 2, 1983.*

before he lapsed into a coma. By October 31, 1983, the death-watch had begun. Virginia kept vigil at her father's bedside with Luckman, Notaro, secretary Ruth Hughes, and Jim Dooley, who Halas had personally rehired in 1981 (at Luckman's behest) to break down game films and help with game planning.

The watch ended at 8:27 PM, when George Halas quietly slipped into the great sleep. Sid Luckman left the vigil to make a prearranged call to the NBC sports office in the Merchandise Mart studio, where the news broke within seconds. Luckman next drove downtown to appear on the 10 PM newscast with Chet Coppock to express his sentiments. Halas dominated the nightly news that evening and the morning papers the next day.

Both Chicago dailies, the *Tribune* and *Sun-Times,* ran special sections leading up to the November 3 funeral. Every league VIP was in attendance, from commissioner Pete Rozelle and the team owners to the Bears themselves. At the request of this man of the people, the Halas funeral was held in his neighborhood parish church, St. Ita's, instead of Holy Name Cathedral downtown.

Tributes came from far and wide. Red Grange, no longer able to travel, had told an interviewer that George Halas had "Guts. He feared no one. He was like a god to me. He was one of the best friends I had in life."

The team, 3–7 a week after the founder died, rallied in a 5–1 closing rush to finish the season with a 23–21 win over the Green Bay Packers, ending up at 8–8. By then, Virginia McCaskey had designated the first person without the Halas name to run the Bears.

THE DITKA BEARS EMERGE

In the 1983–84 off-season, at GM Jerry Vainisi's urging, new Bears president Michael McCaskey ordered the white letters *GSH* woven into the orange stripes on the left sleeve of the uniform jersey as a permanent tribute to the founder. McCaskey also ordered navy blue pants with orange and white vertical stripes down each leg to be worn with the white road jerseys.

Mike Ditka convinced Vainisi to move summer training camp to UW/Platteville in southwestern Wisconsin. He believed this change would establish a businesslike championship atmosphere, as well as team unity, and would take them away from the distractions of home in Lake Forest and the lure of Chicago. With three football fields, a huge dorm and dining hall, meeting rooms, and close proximity to a small

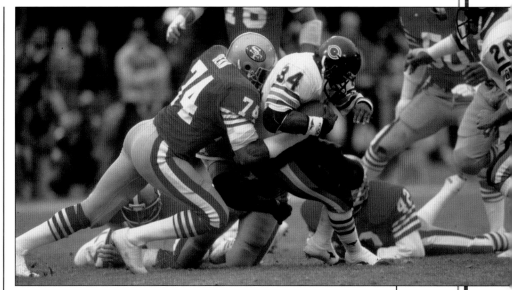

Walter Payton gains a few hard-earned yards as the 49ers win the NFC championship game at Candlestick Park on January 6, 1985.

A GAME AWAY FROM THE SUPER BOWL

Mike Ditka accepts congratulations from Redskins coach Joe Gibbs after the Bears beat Washington in the first playoff round.

The Bears earned an early New Year's gift on December 30, 1984, when they sacked Joe Theismann seven times to beat the Washington Redskins 23–19. "When we tried to go fancy, we got into trouble," said defensive coordinator Buddy Ryan. "So we went back to being mean and nasty." The nastiest hit of all was safety Todd Bell's smashing tackle that KO'd Joe Washington.

Michael McCaskey and Mike Ditka agreed on a contract extension in the week before the game with the 49ers. San Francisco, led by Joe Montana, was too strong, beating down the Bears 23–0. But as Dick Butkus told Jerry Vainisi, "Thank you for making us proud to be Bears again."

downtown bar district where the players could unwind before curfew, this team had access to what it needed to succeed.

In 1984, Jim McMahon was the leader and clutch passer the Bears hadn't seen in nearly two decades. Walter Payton, at age 30, had his best season since he led the league in rushing in 1977. Buddy Ryan's "46 defense" intimidated opponents.

And the Bears proved they were back when they manhandled the defending champion Los Angeles Raiders 17–6 on November 4, 1984, at Soldier Field. Payton scored two first-half touchdowns as the defense caused five turnovers and got nine sacks. Victory came at a season-ending price, however, when McMahon suffered a lacerated kidney in a sandwich between Raider linemen Howie Long and Bill Pickel.

The Bears clinched the NFC Central three weeks later, beating the Minnesota Vikings 34–3. Ending the regular season at 10–6, they had a December 30 date at Washington's RFK Stadium with the defending NFC champion Redskins.

HOW SWEET HE WAS

His teammates called him Sweetness for his accomplishments, wit, and drive. It was a nickname that fit Walter Payton's chiseled 5'10", 200-pound frame—and his unique, impossible-to-define personality—like a tailored suit. Only the irreverent Jim McMahon got away with calling him Wally; to everyone else he was Walter.

Walter Payton was the best-conditioned athlete in the league, and to keep that up, he ran tirelessly up and down a steep hill he built in the northwest suburbs—"Die Hard" was his motto. When he didn't seek out defenders in that distinctive, stiff-legged gait that drew its power from his hips and thighs, he pulverized them with stiff arms and crushing blocks.

Payton loved music—while in college, he came to Chicago and won a national dance contest on the television show *Soul Train.* Ironically enough, he did not play football until his junior year at Columbia High in Mississippi. He acquiesced only because his coach, Charles Boston, let him play drums in the school band as well as star on the field.

In his four seasons at Jackson State, Payton gained 3,563 yards and scored an NCAA-record 464 points on 68 touchdowns, five field goals, and 53 extra points. With the Bears, he set a National Football League rushing record—16,726 yards—that lasted for 18 years. That total does not include the 632 yards Payton gained in nine playoff games.

> WALTER PAYTON WAS THE BEST-CONDITIONED ATHLETE IN THE LEAGUE, AND TO KEEP THAT UP, HE RAN TIRELESSLY UP AND DOWN A STEEP HILL HE BUILT IN THE NORTHWEST SUBURBS—"DIE HARD" WAS HIS MOTTO.

Walter Payton scores one of his three touchdowns as the Bears beat the St. Louis Cardinals 42–6 to gain the playoffs. Their December 16, 1979, win at Soldier Field honored the memory of Mugs Halas, who died during the night from a massive heart attack.

WALTER PAYTON'S RECORDS

Walter Payton held 16 NFL records when he retired, along with 27 additional Bears records. The most prominent was the 16,726-yard career rushing mark that held until Emmitt Smith surpassed it in 2002. Payton set that yardage record on 3,838 carries and ran for a record 110 touchdowns among his career 125, tying for ninth in NFL history. He caught 492 passes for 4,538 yards and 15 more touchdowns. He is third on the all-time list for total combined yards: 21,803. The record he set in 1977, with his 275-yard rushing game against Minnesota, lasted for 23 years.

For the Bears, he is far and away the all-time rushing leader, more than 10,000 yards ahead of Neal Anderson, who is second, Rick Casares who is third, and Gale Sayers, who is fourth.

Walter Payton vaults high over various Lions defenders.

Drafted as the fourth overall pick in 1975, Payton quickly established his credentials. "He thinks he has to carry the team on his shoulders," said Payton's first pro coach Jack Pardee. "He has a great sense of loyalty."

That loyalty was shown in Payton's 1993 induction speech at the Pro Football Hall of Fame. "Every guy, every offensive lineman that played for the Chicago Bears helped me get that 16,000, and I thank them."

General manager Jim Finks knew Payton's worth. When Payton led the league in 1977 with 1,852 yards and 16 touchdowns and won the league's Most Valuable Player Award, Finks said, "He is a complete football player. He is better than Jim Brown. He is better than O. J. Simpson."

The career rushing record came against the New Orleans Saints on October 7, 1984, when he took off on a six-yard sweep around the left end to surpass Jim Brown's record 12,312 yards. When Walter bounced up with the record carry in hand, the officials handed the ball to Pro Football Hall of Fame executive director Pete Elliott, who dispatched it to Canton for display.

In 1985, his eleventh season, Payton at age 31—old for a running back—gained 1,551 yards, scored 11 touchdowns, and passed for another to lead the Bears to the world championship in Super Bowl XX. But after 13 NFL seasons, Payton hurt all over. He had missed only one game, in 1975, from his rookie season to his retirement in 1987.

Walter Payton was emotional—he might laugh, or he might weep. He broke down at Soldier Field after the final gun ended his last home game. He cried when his son, Jarrett, introduced him at his induction into the Pro Football Hall of Fame. Nobody knew if they were tears of sadness or tears of joy. That was the wonderful mystery of the man called Sweetness.

Convoyed behind guards Kurt Becker (79) and Mark Bortz (62), Walter Payton (34) breaks Jim Brown's NFL rushing record in a 20–7 victory over the New Orleans Saints on October 7, 1984, at Soldier Field. Payton's record remained unbroken until it was surpassed by Emmitt Smith in 2002.

BEST OF THE BEARS

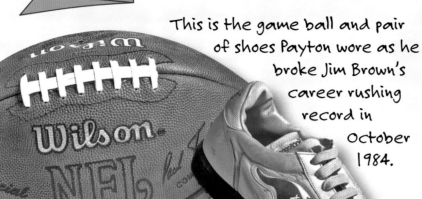

This is the game ball and pair of shoes Payton wore as he broke Jim Brown's career rushing record in October 1984.

Payton often wore this towel tucked into the front of his uniform.

Walter Payton's bobblehead features his total rushing yards.

In 1976, Payton won the Willie Galimore Memorial Award for NFC Veteran of the Year.

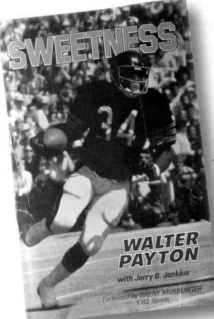

Sweetness, a biography of Walter Payton, was published in 1980.

SWEETNESS

WALTER PAYTON

with Jerry B. Jenkins

Foreword by BRENT MUSBURGER
CBS Sports

WALTER PAYTON
ALL-TIME RUSHING LEADER
16,726 TOTAL YARDS

Every player enshrined in the Pro Football Hall of Fame receives a ring; Payton recieved his in 1993.

Payton earned NFL MVP honors in 1977.

Payton's Hall of Fame bust now resides at Walter Payton's Roundhouse in Aurora, Illinois.

The *Pure Payton* VHS tape, released in 1977, features game highlights and clips from his Bears seasons.

The iconic and beloved number 34 jersey worn by Walter Payton is the most popular jersey in team history.

Payton was presented with this ball for his record 275-yard game against the Vikings in 1977.

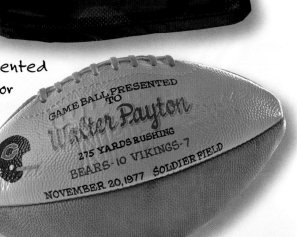

SOLDIER FIELD GETS SKYBOXES AND REAL GRASS

Back in 1980, on the eve of the final preseason game, the Bears' lease on Soldier Field had been within hours of expiring. Mayor Jane Byrne had dispatched a messenger with a contract renewal to the Bears' 55 East Jackson offices. When he read the cover letter, then-controller Jerry Vainisi realized

September 2, 1979, was opening day at Soldier Field. The Bears beat the Green Bay Packers 6–3 on a pair of Bob Thomas field goals. Mike Phipps led the team to a 7–1 stretch drive to make the playoffs with a 10–6 record.

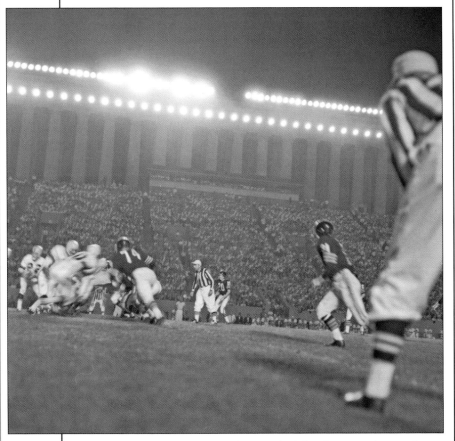

With lights blazing, Soldier Field is packed for the Annual Armed Forces Game on September 16, 1960. The Bears, including defenders Bob Kilcullen (74), Justin Rowland (20), Erich Barnes (24), and Harlon Hill (87), beat Bobby Layne (22) and the Pittsburgh Steelers in the exhibition finale 21–10.

the mayor meant business. She had given the Bears 24 hours to sign it or be evicted.

"We were forced to sign a 20-year lease," said Vainisi when he was interviewed for the biography *Papa Bear: The Life and Legacy of George Halas.* With a figurative gun to their heads, Vainisi and George Halas went to City Hall the next day and signed the deal, but not before the city agreed to give the Bears the right to build and control skyboxes.

The Bears had to pay for the construction of the boxes, as well as take all the risks, but ultimately it was a winner for the

By 1981, Soldier Field had undergone significant remodeling, with the addition of skyboxes on each side of the field and permanent concrete stands at the north end. However, the stadium was still unsatisfactory, forcing the renovation that came in 2002.

team. Once the costs were amortized, the Bears would receive 80 percent of the revenues. The park district would get the other 20 percent.

Thus, skyboxes became lucrative cash cows for the McCaskeys, as they were for every other team in sports that had them. But the McCaskeys needed that skybox money. The park district charged the Bears the highest rent in the league—by 1985, the team's rental fee was about $4 million a year.

The playing field was another matter. Since the Bears had moved into Soldier Field in 1971, they had played on an artificial surface that got harder and harder as the years went by,

and it became more slippery as it wore down. On rainy days, anything could—and usually did—happen, to the detriment of the team.

The players in Chicago and throughout the league had wanted natural grass in all the stadiums for years. In 1988, the Bears finally got their sod back. But because the playing area at Soldier Field is barely above the water table, the footing after rainfall was horrible, if not outright dangerous. Later in the season, when high school teams held playoff games there and the weather got cold, the playing field developed ruts, which still holds true today.

THE INCOMPARABLE SUPER SEASON

The 1985 Chicago Bears stand on their own. For one magical season, the Bears intimidated and dominated the league. They scored 456 points, including four defensive touchdowns, two kickoff runbacks, and two safeties. They stormed through the playoffs in controlled fury as they

The "Junkyard Dogs" attack in Super Bowl XX in New Orleans on January 26, 1986. Referee Red Cashion watches Otis Wilson sack New England's Steve Grogan as Richard Dent (95) and Dan Hampton (99) are ready to assist. The Bears got seven sacks in the 46–10 rout.

mutilated the New York Giants, Los Angeles Rams, and New England Patriots by a combined 91 points to 10.

Two season-long holdouts might have destroyed any other team. Linebacker Al Harris would not bend in his demands. When management let Todd Bell, the linchpin of the "46 defense," stay out, Buddy Ryan was irate. Jerry Vainisi, though, supplied Ryan with two outstanding replacements to plug into his scheme: 1984's top pick, linebacker Wilber Marshall, and safety Dave Duerson.

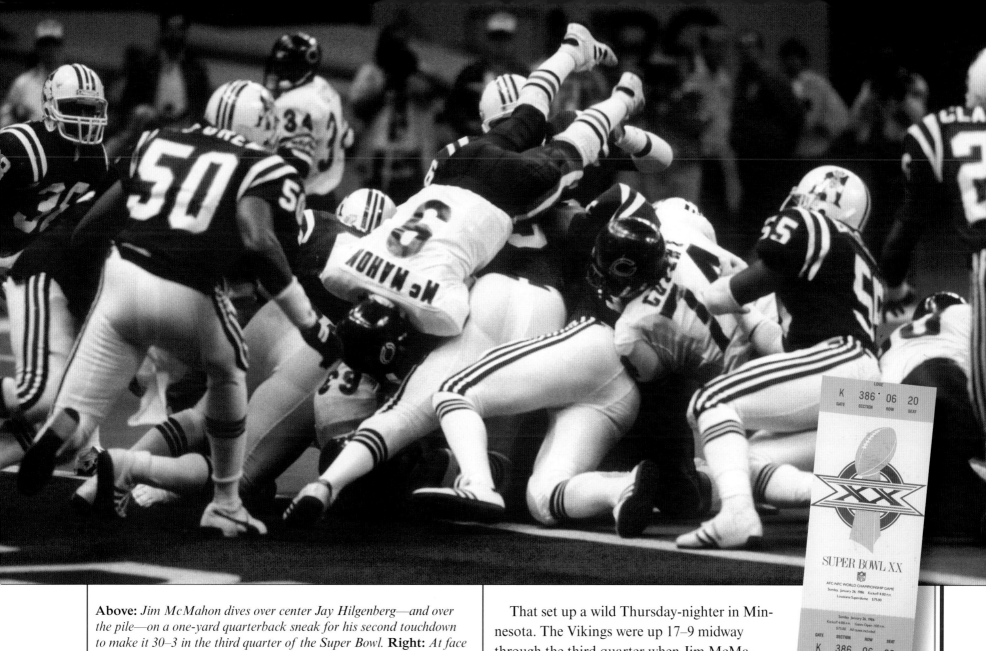

Above: *Jim McMahon dives over center Jay Hilgenberg—and over the pile—on a one-yard quarterback sneak for his second touchdown to make it 30–3 in the third quarter of the Super Bowl.* **Right:** *At face value, a ticket to Super Bowl XX at the Louisiana Superdome cost $75, but the hard-to-get tickets were scalped for much more.*

The keynote for the season was sounded early in the third quarter of the home opener against Tampa Bay. With the Bears trailing 28–17, Richard Dent tipped a Steve DeBerg pass, and Leslie Frazier grabbed it to race 29 yards for the score. Two more touchdowns iced the 38–28 victory. A week later, the New England Patriots came to town and went home whipped after losing 20–7.

That set up a wild Thursday-nighter in Minnesota. The Vikings were up 17–9 midway through the third quarter when Jim McMahon, who had been hospitalized with an upper back/neck injury, badgered Mike Ditka to let him play. Ditka relented, and McMahon lit the fire. On his first play, he dropped back, Walter Payton applied a crushing block, and the punky QB fired a bomb to Willie Gault, who caught it in stride for a 70-yard touchdown. On the next possession, McMahon completed the first of two consecutive touchdown passes to Dennis McKinnon. The Bears led 30–17 after yet another touchdown, then added a Kevin Butler field goal to return home with a 33–24 victory. "Incredible," running back Matt Suhey said to reporter Kevin Lamb. "I've never seen anything like it."

Ten days later, back in Chicago, the Bears spotted the Washington Redskins a 10–0 lead and then cut loose with a remarkable 45 unanswered points, set off by Gault's 99-yard kickoff runback. Then McMahon took charge with touchdown passes to McKinnon and Emery Moorehead. Out of the shotgun, McMahon handed off to Payton, who fired deep to a wide-open McMahon for the touchdown. McMahon returned the favor with a scoring pass to Payton in the third quarter as the Bears won 45–10. America began to take notice.

Next, the Bears marched into San Francisco's Candlestick Park and took a 26–10 victory. In the January playoff game the previous year, Bill Walsh had inserted guard Guy McIntyre into the backfield and had him carry the ball. Not to be outdone, Ditka called on 308-pound rookie defensive tackle William "The Refrigerator" Perry, who ran twice for four yards to finish the game.

That was just Perry's warm-up—he broke loose on a Monday night in Chicago against the Packers. Inserted into the goal line attack in the second quarter, he bulldozed Green Bay's George Cumby to clear the first of two touchdown paths for Payton. Four minutes later, Ditka had McMahon give Perry the ball from a yard out, and the Fridge became an instant American hero when he scored. The Bears won 23–7 and remained unbeaten after seven games.

Two weeks later, the return match at Green Bay featured Packer late hits and muggings against Payton, McMahon, and Matt Suhey and plenty of return blasts from the Bears. "They don't like us, and we don't like them," Ditka said of rival coach Forrest Gregg and the team. The crowd roared when Perry entered the game, went in motion, and caught McMahon's four-yard pass in stride in the end zone. Payton's 27-yard touchdown run clinched a 16–10 win that Mike Singletary called "Nasty. Our kind of football!"

McMahon sat out for a month with a shoulder injury, and Steve Fuller took his place. In Game 11, the Bears marched into Dallas and played as close to a perfect game as the league had seen since the 73–0 title romp in 1940. The defense never let the Cowboys closer than the Chicago 38-yard line. Fuller's crisp passes and Payton's 132 yards on the ground finished a 44–0 victory as the Bears clinched NFC home field advantage.

The Bears' 12–0 unbeaten campaign ended two weeks later on a hot Monday night in Miami, when the Dolphins did everything right, got all the breaks, and walked away with a 38–24 victory, despite McMahon's return in the second half. Finally, at 15–1, it was time to dial up the big push, starting with the New York Giants on January 5, 1986.

The Bears pitched a shutout in strong winds and bitter cold at Soldier Field. The defense stifled the Giants, led by Dent's three and a half sacks against Phil Simms. "Old-fashioned football," said Mike Ditka. The Bears' halftime lead was 7–0 when New York's Sean Landeta barely ticked the ball, and Shaun Gayle picked it up and ran in from five yards out.

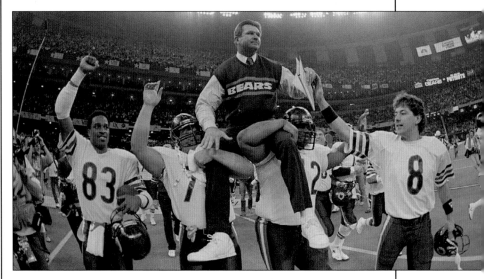

Above: *Steve McMichael and William Perry carry coach Mike Ditka off the Louisiana Superdome turf after the Bears win Super Bowl XX. Willie Gault (83) and Maury Buford (8) join the escort.* **Left:** *The Highland Mint issued a 24k gold coin in honor of Super Bowl XX.*

THE SUPER BOWL SHUFFLE

As the Bears roared through their Super Bowl season, record producer Randy Weigand asked his girlfriend, Honey Bear Courtney Larson, if she would introduce him to wide receiver Willie Gault. Weigand told Gault he had a great marketing promotion in mind: He would use the players in a song and video called *The Super Bowl Shuffle*. Bobby Daniels and Lloyd Barry wrote the song, and Dick Meyer and Melvin Owens penned the lyrics.

THE SUPER BOWL SHUFFLE*
THE CHICAGO BEARS SHUFFLIN' CREW

"A substantial portion of the proceeds from this record will be donated to help feed Chicago's neediest families.

Most of the team chose to participate, with Dan Hampton as one of the exceptions—he thought the whole thing was too over the top. They recorded it at the Park West in Lincoln Park on the Tuesday after they lost to the Dolphins in Game 13 in Miami. The Walter Payton and Jim McMahon solos were edited into the video later because they missed the original shoot.

The song/video was nominated for a Grammy and sold nearly a million copies. Profits went to charity, substantiating Payton's solo claim that "We're not doing this because we're greedy, the Bears are doing it to feed the needy."

McMahon finished it in the third quarter with a pair of touchdown passes to Dennis McKinnon for a 21–0 final score.

The Bears showed the Los Angeles Rams why they were the 11-point favorites in the NFC championship game when they held Eric Dickerson to 46 yards and caused him to fumble twice. McMahon ran 16 yards for the first Bears touchdown, diving into the end zone from 2 yards out to score. In the third quarter, McMahon rolled left, jumped, and threw against his body to Gault in the end zone, a 22-yard scoring pass that made it 17–0. Late in the game, Marshall picked up a Dieter Brock fumble and ran 52 yards to put away the 24–0 victory. Hence, the Bears had Super Bowl reservations in New Orleans against the New England Patriots.

The Bears cut a swath through the Crescent City the entire Super Bowl week, executing a display of dominating defense and irresistible offense. Dent settled the issue early in the game when he forced Tony Eason and Craig James to fumble, giving the Bears a 13–3 lead after one quarter. By halftime it was 23–3, then, after Perry crashed the end zone, 44–3. Henry Wachter trapped the Patriots' Steve Grogan in the end zone for a safety, garnering a final 46–10 result that Bear fans still savor, though Ditka and McMahon both regretted they did not get Payton a touchdown. When it ended, the players carried coaches Ditka and Ryan off the field.

At least a million people jammed downtown Chicago in below-zero weather to see the team's parade to the Daley Civic Center. By then, Ryan was the head coach of the Philadelphia Eagles. Later, Singletary told reporter Lamb that he didn't want people to remember the '85 Bears as a pretty good team. He wanted them to say, "They were the best. Not just of 1985, but the best of all time." Who's to argue?

Bears president Michael McCaskey holds up the Vince Lombardi trophy in celebration of Chicago's Super Bowl–champion Bears on January 27, 1986, at the Daley Civic Center. An estimated one million fans braved the bitter cold to honor the team.

DOMINANT DEFENSE

Which defensive unit was better: 1985 or 1986? It's hard to argue against 1985, the only Super Bowl winner in Bears history. When it came to the numbers, the '85 Bear defense ranked first overall, as well as in rush defense and in points allowed. It was also a colorful and quotable unit that displayed utter dominance of the league and in the playoffs—they walked the walk after they talked the talk in *The Super Bowl Shuffle.* Finally, the irascible, controversial defensive coordinator Buddy Ryan, who was engaged in a duel he could not win with head coach Mike Ditka, led them. Together they were fire, with results.

Yet the 1986 unit fared better, with far less controversy, under soft-spoken new coordinator Vince Tobin, brother of Bears' personnel director Bill Tobin. Unlike the 1985 defense that seemed to operate in high gear—in takeaway mode at all times—this one often played it safer. The 1986 Bear offense was not as potent. Jim McMahon was hurt much of the

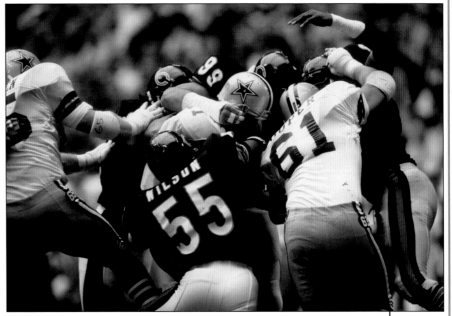

Dan Hampton (99) and Otis Wilson (55) engulf Dallas quarterback Danny White at Texas Stadium on November 17, 1985. The Bears overwhelmed the Cowboys 44–0 in the defining game for the "46" defense. America realized that this was the team that would win the Super Bowl.

DEFENSIVE MILESTONES

The most significant milestone for any defense is the number 0. The '85 Bear defense pitched two regular-season shutouts and two more in the playoffs.

The spree began when they routed the Cowboys 44–0 at Texas Stadium, a game that included two defensive touchdowns. Richard Dent scored on Dan Hampton's tipped interception. Mike Richardson did it on a 36-yard runback.

A week later, they held the Atlanta Falcons to –22 passing yards in a 36–0 shutout at Soldier Field. "They must have felt like it was Sherman's Army marching through them," Mike Ditka said.

Combine that with the 21–0 playoff shutout over the Giants and a 24–0 rout of the Rams, and the '85 Bears finished with four shutouts among their 18 victories.

season, and the defense—after the fourth game, a 44–7 rout of Cincinnati—took over more of the burden. McMahon was knocked out for the season with a shoulder tear in Game 12 when Green Bay's Charles Martin threw him to the Soldier Field turf from behind, forcing Jerry Vainisi to sign 1984 Heisman winner Doug Flutie.

The '86 Bear defense ranked first in total yardage allowed but second in rushing and passing yardage. They finished their 14–2 campaign by allowing a miserly league-record 187 points, just 11.7 points per game. The disappointment came in the January 3, 1987, playoff game when the Redskins stymied quarterback Doug Flutie and clubbed their way through the Bear defense to a 27–13 victory, ending the magnificent run.

BUDDY RYAN AND HIS HEROES

Buddy Ryan won his first Super Bowl ring as defensive line coach with the 1968 New York Jets. He went to the Minnesota Vikings in 1973 and came to Chicago in 1978 as defensive coordinator, with Neill Armstrong as head coach. Defense was the Bears' hallmark then. Aware that Armstrong would be fired after the 1981 season, the defensive players signed a letter to Halas at season's end, urging Papa Bear to retain Ryan. Impressed by the players' loyalty and Ryan's intellectual strength, Halas kept him, gave him a raise, and told new head coach Mike Ditka that Ryan would be there.

Ryan created and implemented his attacking "46 defense" with the Bears. "We're not good enough to rush just four linemen, or a linebacker or two," Ryan said on *Bears Bound for Glory,* shown on WMAQ-TV the night before Super Bowl XX. "We need seven or even eight men on our blitzes." Ryan taught his defense to attack, read on the fly, and react. The strong safety was the key to Ryan's "46." He had to be quick enough to cover a wide receiver, strong enough to handle a tight end, and tough enough to act as a fourth linebacker. Doug Plank wore the original number 46; he was followed by Todd Bell, a fellow Ohio State alum who held out in 1985; and next came his substitute, Dave Duerson, who retained the job after Ryan left in 1986.

Ditka and Ryan barely coexisted through the first 12 games in 1985. On December 2, at halftime, after Miami's Dan Marino torched the "46 defense" with short, quick passes for a 31–10 lead, Ditka and Ryan nearly came to blows when Ryan refused to adjust. Ryan gave in and finally adapted, and the Bears came close, losing their only game that season 38–24.

By Saturday night of Super Bowl week, Ryan's imminent departure was common knowledge. In his final meeting with the defense, a tearful Ryan told them, "You are my heroes." They responded the next day with the most dominant performance in pro football history as the Bears and their "46 defense" won by the fitting final score of 46–10.

Then it was off to Philadelphia for Ryan, where he coached until 1990. He finished with a job in Houston and then in Arizona before he was fired by the Cardinals in 1996. Ditka and Ryan carried on a nasty feud long after their Chicago days together as the Bears battled the Eagles season after season. Early in the 21st century, however, the two coaches realized something: Over the years, their rivalry fueled them and eventually became the key to their individual success. The feud was finally over.

Defensive team captain Mike Singletary goes over plays with defensive coordinator Buddy Ryan before a 1984 game against the Detroit Lions.

The November 23, 1985, *Sports Illustrated* cover says a thousand words after the Bears beat Dallas.

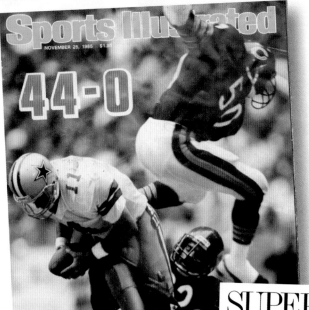

On January 27, 1986, the *Chicago Tribune* shows Mike Ditka and Buddy Ryan being carried off the field at the Louisiana Superdome following the Bears' 46–10 Super Bowl XX win over the Patriots.

Chicago Tribune

25¢ City and suburbs/35¢ elsewhere

Super Bowl Final

Monday, January 27, 1986

Bears bring it home

By Phil Hersh
Chicago Tribune

NEW ORLEANS—It is a good thing Chicago is the city of the big shoulders. How else could it Bear up to the task of carrying an entire football team in a victory parade from here to eternity?

Sporting immortality is where the Chicago Bears are headed. They proved you can get there from New Orleans in a day trip.

With a 46-10 victory over the New England Patriots in Sunday's Super Bowl XX at the Louisiana Superdome, the Bears also took the entire city on a long-awaited joyride. They found the way to get over the hump that had always overturned the civic bandwagon, littering the streets with broken dreams instead of confetti.

Twenty-three years have passed since the 1963 Bears won Chicago's last title in a major professional sport. At last, the Second City can chant "We're No. 1" without fear of flying too high.

With only a few minutes—but no doubt—left in the game, the bitterly cold streets up north in Chicago began to fill with warm bodies and the sound of car horns. Fans across the city gravitated toward the Rush Street area, and once the game was over, auto traffic on the Near North Side was at a standstill. Pedestrian traffic was little better.

In the Loop, those who braved the frozen Daley Plaza danced in the cold as the "Super Bowl Shuffle" played larger than life on the giant screen behind them.

Bears' head coach Mike Ditka was speaking of them—and hundreds of thousands of other people like them, football players and fans alike—when he told his victory press conference that "A lot of dreams have been fulfilled, and a lot of frustrations have ended."

The Bears, once hoisted aloft, can simply put one foot on the Picasso, another on the Sears Tower and step right up to the Chicago cloud, where team founder George Halas will be waiting. Or they say do the route linebacker Mike Singletary has mapped out.

"I'm so happy," Singletary said, "I feel like I could jump on top of the Superdome."

field, defensive coordinator Buddy Ryan confirms what the Patriots learned Sunday—the Bears are No. 1 in the NFL.

Tribune photo by Ed Wagner Jr.

Overdue to overdone

...er had cheered Grange decades ...a Sunday, he cheered Payton too. ...cent in the Oak Park Arms Hotel, 408 ...Park Ave., in Oak Park, where he ...years younger than the oldest man

sons grinned at each other as they rolled the taste of "Chicago Bears, Super Bowl Champions" around on their tongues.

But Bourbon Street in New Orleans and Rush Street here bore the brunt of the

Full coverage

● It was no contest Sunday—the Bears are the NFL's best.
● The Bears can dry, says Bernie Lincicome. Chicago has a champ.
● No sweat, says Bob Verdi. The Bears are as good as their ton...

SUPER BOWL XX

The Official Super Bowl XX Game Program

$5.00

Chicago Bears vs.
New England Patriots

AFC vs. NFC for the NFL Championship and the Vince Lombardi Trophy   Sunday, January 26, 1986 4:00 P.M. Louisiana Superdome

This is the official program for Super Bowl XX on January 26, 1986, at the Louisiana Superdome in New Orleans.

Each Bears team member received this diamond-studded Super Bowl ring that declared them the 1985 world champions.

Wilber Marshall, Dan Hampton, Otis Wilson, and Mike Singletary had just attacked Patriots quarterback Tony Eason on this *Sports Illustrated* cover from February 3, 1986.

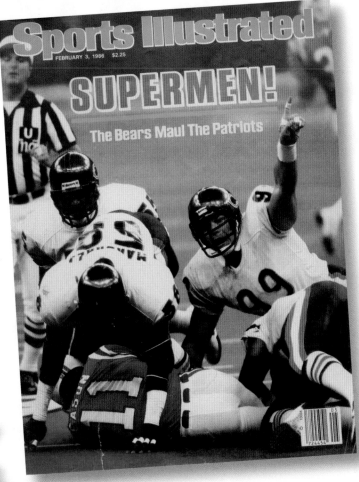

Jim McMahon and Walter Payton are dressed to kill, portraying their Chicago version of the popular '80s television show *Miami Vice*.

This pin's attachment reminds everyone of the Bears' Super Bowl XX win.

A 1985 world champions pennant is a souvenir for the ages!

STARS OF THE DITKA ERA

No team since the beginning of the television era had a more stellar cast of characters and talent than the Bears of the '80s. Carefully assembled by general managers Jim Finks and Jerry Vainisi, the team was tailored to the driving personality of coach Mike Ditka and to surround and enhance the greatness of Walter Payton.

Jim McMahon was the first player Mike Ditka selected in the 1982 draft. The Bears won five straight divisional titles and Super Bowl XX during McMahon's tenure.

Ditka's first draft choice in 1982 was **Jim McMahon**—the flamboyant leader and swashbuckling quarterback who drove the bus. From the last three games McMahon played in 1984, through 15 starts in 1985, six in 1986 before he was knocked out for the season, and two more in 1987, the Bears went 26–0. McMahon left after 1988, injured and furious at Bears owner Michael McCaskey, whom he blamed for the team's failure to win more than a single Super Bowl. He finished his career in Green Bay, backing up Brett Favre.

The great defense featured Hall of Famers Mike Singletary and Dan Hampton. Richard Dent is another who might make the Hall. Offensive linemen Jay Hilgenberg and Jim Covert would have been locks for the Hall if they had played for another franchise.

Middle linebacker **Mike Singletary** was the heart and soul of the defense. He was a player so driven and consistent that Buddy Ryan

Future Hall of Famers Dan Hampton (99) and team captain Mike Singletary (50) leave the field feeling victorious after beating Philadelphia 20–12 in "The Fog Bowl" on New Year's Eve 1988.

called him the best player in the National Football League. He was named to the Pro Bowl ten times. Singletary was promoted to head coach of the San Francisco 49ers in 2008, and he began reviving the team.

Dan Hampton, the tackle and defensive end from Arkansas, was an extraordinary physical specimen with an acute sense of the game's intricacies. He played in four Pro Bowls. Hampton, a purist, decided not to participate in *The Super Bowl Shuffle.* He defended his decision by saying, "Anytime you start patting yourself on the back, you got only one hand to play with." Today, the "Danimal" watches the team closely as a Chicago radio analyst.

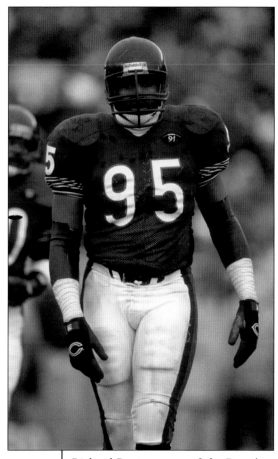

Richard Dent was one of the Bears' greatest players for more than a decade. He was the last man from the Ditka era to play in the Pro Bowl.

Richard Dent fell to the eighth round in the 1983 draft but played himself into immediate stardom. He was a superior pass rusher and the Most Valuable Player of Super Bowl XX, in a you-pick-it scenario that could have gone to several others, including McMahon, Singletary, Hampton, or Steve McMichael. Dent was a four-time Pro Bowler.

Four other Ditka-era Bears could make the Hall someday, most likely as old-timers. Center **Jay Hilgenberg,** a free agent from the Iowa family of great centers, anchored the offensive line that cleared the way for the top rushing attack in the league. A seven-time Pro Bowler, he played 11 seasons for the Bears and 2 more in Cleveland and New Orleans.

Defensive tackle **Steve McMichael** holds the team record of 191 consecutive games; he did it in 13 seasons from 1981 to 1993. "Mongo" spent 1994 in Green Bay, where he played in 16 more games for an amazing total of 207. Immediately after that season, he returned to Chicago, where he and his family live. McMichael was a larger-than-life character then and remains one to this day. He played in two Pro Bowls.

Jim Covert was a gentle giant off the field. He was an English major at Pitt, where he also happened to be a hard-nosed, tough, and highly skilled left tackle on offense. As long as Jimbo was healthy, and he was from 1983 until 1988 when he hurt his back, the Bears had the best running game in the league. He was named to the NFL's team of the '80s. The great New York Giants outside linebacker Lawrence Taylor was no match for Covert when they met in the 1985 playoffs and again in the '87 opener.

Gary Fencik, a native of Barrington, Illinois, got his education at Yale and his football education in Chicago under Buddy Ryan. He was a superb free safety, a sure tackler, and is the Bears' all-time leading interceptor with 38 picks. The articulate Fencik served as an analyst on NBC's Channel 5 *Sports Sunday* telecast in the 1980s.

No discussion of this team would be complete without mentioning **William "The Refrigerator" Perry**. The Fridge, from Clemson, was Chicago's first pick of the 1985 draft. Ditka and his conditioning staff brought

Jim Covert was the sixth pick in the 1983 draft's first round; he anchored the Bears' offensive line throughout the '80s. During his career, he was named to the All-Pro team for four straight years (1984–1987).

him down to a svelte 308 pounds. As big as he was, Perry was graceful, had superb footwork, could jump high enough to dunk a basketball, and was unbelievably strong. Once he started carrying the ball, his phone rang off the hook with offers. "I call him the endorser," Hampton said.

"I'm just having fun," said the ever-smiling Fridge. And the rest of America agreed wholeheartedly.

THE DESTRUCTIVE STRIKE OF 1987

Everything was set for the Bears to reclaim the throne in 1987. They pulled out all the stops against the Giants in a Monday Night opener for a 34–19 win. Mike Tomczak, who started for Jim McMahon while he was recovering from shoulder surgery, passed for 292 yards to lead a 416-yard attack, and the Bears totaled nine sacks. A week later, they dispatched Tampa Bay 20–3. And then the players went on strike.

Captain and union rep Mike Singletary kept his Bears in line. Not one crossed the picket line for the "replacement" games. Ditka cajoled two wins out of the "Spare Bears," as the media called them, and then popped off. "These are the *real* Bears," the coach said. They lost a week later to New Orleans.

The regulars returned on October 25 against Tampa Bay, as did McMahon—he came off the bench with the Bears

Sean Payton (17) was a quarterback for the "Spare Bears"—the team that crossed the regulars' picket lines in the 1987 strike season. Payton eventually became coach of the New Orleans Saints.

WALTER PAYTON DAY

It was a bittersweet day: On December 20, 1987, Walter Payton said farewell to Soldier Field fans. Sweetness played his best game of the season as he gained 79 yards and scored two touchdowns, but the Seattle Seahawks had an answer for every salvo and won 34–21.

The team honored Payton before the game. "When you finish playing for the Chicago Bears, number 34 will be retired," Bears president Michael McCaskey said. "You are the greatest running back ever to play the game of football. Walter, we love you. Thank you for enriching our lives."

Payton is recognized on "Walter Payton Day," December 20, 1987, the day of his last regular-season home game.

12 points down and led them to victory in the final six minutes. He scored on a quarterback sneak and threw a six-yard touchdown pass to Neal Anderson, sewing up a 27–26 win.

Then the Bears went flat. They lost 41–0 to the 49ers on a Monday night before Ditka threw his chewing gum at a fan. A week later, Seattle came to Chicago and went away with a 34–21 win in Walter Payton's last regular-season game. The Bears were ousted in the playoff opener at Soldier Field when Washington's Darrell Green ran back a punt 52 yards for a 21–17 win, and the season reflected Ditka's early October comment. "With those words, Mike Ditka lost the team," Singletary said years later. "It was never the same."

BEST RECORD, NO SUPER BOWL

When 1988 rolled around, several familiar Chicago Bear faces were gone. Walter Payton had just retired. Jerry Vainisi had been gone a year after Michael McCaskey fired him in a dispute that Commissioner Pete Rozelle ultimately settled in Vainisi's favor. Lacking Vainisi's wise counsel, McCaskey, wearing a second hat as general manager, let stellar outside linebacker Wilber Marshall slip away as a free agent—McCaskey refused to match the Washington Redskins' million-dollar offer.

Regardless, the Bears were again poised for greatness. The defense was suffocating opponents on a regular basis, and Neal Anderson was developing into the next great Chicago running back after two years as Payton's understudy. The defense held six of its first eight opponents to single-digit scoring, and Anderson didn't appear to be bothered by inconsistent play at quarterback.

The San Francisco 49ers came to town at the season's midpoint for a Monday night date. The big play in the Bears' 10–9 victory came when Richard Dent leaped over blocker Bubba Parris to sack Joe Montana. The Bears were now 7–1, and Super Bowl talk was as hot as it was back in that legendary season of 1985.

But just nine games into the season, the city was stunned when Mike Ditka was hospitalized with a mild heart attack. Ditka's doctor let him accompany the team to Washington in Week 11 to sit on the bench while Vince Tobin handled the team for a second straight week. The Bears made life easy for the coach with a 34–14 win over the defending Super Bowl champions. Ditka awarded game balls to the entire offensive line, whose blocks gave Mike Tomczak time to ring up 229 yards passing and also paved the way for 145 more yards rushing, which were highlighted by Anderson's 50-yard touchdown dash. "It was payback," said safety Dave Duerson. "And payback is a mighty thing."

Anderson's 80-yard touchdown run in the third quarter broke open a tight battle with Green Bay in Week 13, as the Bears won 16–0 to go 11–2. However, the victory proved costly, as Dent broke an ankle and Mike Tomczak suffered a left-shoulder separation—he joined fellow signal caller Jim McMahon on the sideline. That left the quarterbacking duties to untested third-stringer Jim Harbaugh.

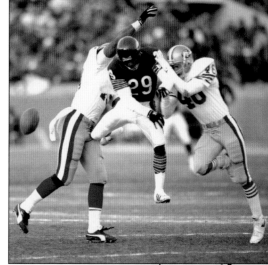

The Bears' Dennis Gentry (29) attempts to catch a pass but is thwarted by 49ers Jeff Fuller (49) and Tom Holmoe (46) during the first quarter of the NFC championship game on January 8, 1989 at Soldier Field.

The Bears lurched down the home stretch with two losses in their last three games; they finished the regular season at 12–4, but they still had home-field advantage throughout the NFC playoffs. And despite the injuries, the Bears entered the postseason as favorites to win their second Super Bowl title in four years.

In a bitter battle with former defensive coordinator Buddy Ryan, who had finally gotten the Eagles back into the playoffs after leaving Chicago to take the head job in Philly following the '85 season, the Bears defeated their former assistant coach 20–12. But in the conference championship game, Montana and the 49ers must have learned something from their defeat at Soldier Field back in Week 8. Montana threw three touchdown passes—two to Jerry Rice in the first half—and the defense completely shut down Chicago's attack. San Francisco stunned the Bears 28–3 en route to the organization's third Super Bowl ring.

BEST OF THE BEARS

This pennant celebrates Jim McMahon, the Chicago Bears' punky quarterback.

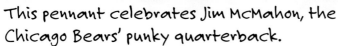

This trading card was signed by Bears great Mike Singletary.

MIKE SINGLETARY LB

Nobody can deny the Bears kept it clean. The 1985 Bears showed up everywhere—even on bars of soap.

Hampton signed his Topps trading card.

BEARS DE **DAN HAMPTON**

HAMPTON 99 GSH

Dan Hampton autographed his jersey with the year of his induction into the Pro Football Hall of Fame, 2002.

The feature story in the Sports section of the *Chicago Sun-Times* on January 15, 2002, has Bears and Eagles players rehash "The Fog Bowl" of December 31, 1988.

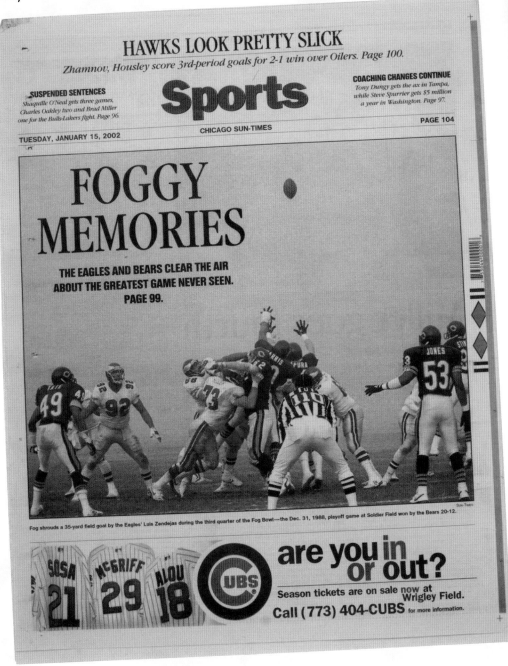

Zhamnov, Housley score 3rd-period goals for 2-1 win over Oilers. Page 100.

SUSPENDED SENTENCES
Shaquille O'Neal gets three games, Charles Oakley two and Brad Miller one for the Bulls-Lakers fight. Page 96.

Sports

COACHING CHANGES CONTINUE
Tony Dungy gets the ax in Tampa, while Steve Spurrier gets $5 million a year in Washington. Page 97.

CHICAGO SUN-TIMES

TUESDAY, JANUARY 15, 2002

PAGE 104

FOGGY MEMORIES

THE EAGLES AND BEARS CLEAR THE AIR ABOUT THE GREATEST GAME NEVER SEEN.
PAGE 99.

Fog shrouds a 35-yard field goal by the Eagles' Luis Zendejas during the third quarter of the Fog Bowl—the Dec. 31, 1988, playoff game at Soldier Field won by the Bears 20-12.

SOSA 21 McGRIFF 29 ALOU 18 CUBS

are you in or out?

Season tickets are on sale now at Wrigley Field.
Call (773) 404-CUBS for more information.

The Fridge shows his true size on the back of "The Refrigerator" & the Monsters of the Midway: William Perry and the Chicago Bears, by Brian Hewitt.

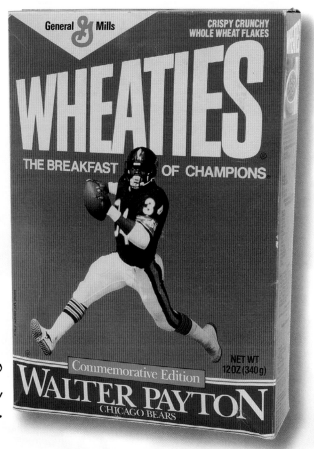

In 1986, Walter Payton became the first football player to be depicted on a Wheaties box. After his death in 1999, Wheaties issued commemorative editions to honor him.

THE FOG BOWL

Mike Ditka's Bears and Buddy Ryan's Philadelphia Eagles could have used help from Rudolph the red-nosed reindeer to light the way through the fog that enveloped Chicago's lakefront and Soldier Field on New Year's Eve 1988. Nothing else would've worked after the pea soup rolled in off Lake Michigan before halftime, when the Bears were leading 17–6.

The Bears started the scoring in an eerie noontime sun, when Mike Tomczak connected with Dennis McKinnon on a brilliant 64-yard touchdown pass. In the second quarter, Randall Cunningham, who passed for 407 yards but never led the Eagles to the end zone, was stopped fourth and two at the 4-yard line as his first down reach fell a finger's width short.

As both teams slugged it out in the fogbank the rest of the way, the fans in Soldier Field and the national television audience were held captive to the down, distance, and play-by-play account of PA announcer Jim Riebandt, who got his report from the sidelines. "The fog was so bad that I was waiting

Bryan Wagner (15) punts out of danger into the pea soup fog that enveloped Soldier Field before halftime on December 31, 1988. It never lifted; the Bears beat the Philadelphia Eagles 20–12 in a playoff game—christened "The Fog Bowl"—that nobody saw.

for Boris Karloff to come out of the stands," Bears offensive guard Tom Thayer told *The New York Times.*

One writer who abandoned the press box to watch from the Bears bench noted, "I couldn't see much. It was like watching the radio." The game ended in a 20–12 Bears victory.

"This is the best game I've never seen," said 32-year-old fan Tom McKee, who watched from Soldier Field's upper reaches.

Fabled "Bear Weather" blew in from Canada a week later as Bill Walsh's underdog San Francisco 49ers came to town. Led by Joe Montana's passes to Jerry Rice, the Niners were the masters of the icebox as they chilled the Bears' Super Bowl ambitions 28–3.

BAD-WEATHER BEAR GAMES

Miserable weather conditions are all too familiar to Bear fans. The Green Bay Packers were the opposition in five of Chicago's 20 coldest games. The coldest to date was the 2008 home season finale on December 22, when Robbie Gould nailed a 38-yard field goal in overtime, giving the Bears a 20–17 win to keep Chicago playoff hopes alive. The temperature that night was 2 degrees, with a windchill of –13 degrees.

The Bears have played three cold-weather postseason games, most notably the 1963 title game with the Giants, when the windchill factor was –3 degrees. But cold temperatures aren't the only inclement weather condition that Bears fans have faced. Game day on December 12, 1965, brought 54-degree temperatures, heavy rain, and 15-mph winds. However, Gale Sayers still managed to score six touchdowns.

THE INSTANT REPLAY GAME

For years, the 1989 Packers' 14–13 win over the Bears was marked with an asterisk in the Bears' press guide and footnoted as "the instant replay game"—at the order of team president Michael McCaskey. That November 5, 1989, head-knocker at Lambeau Field remains the single most controversial game in the long rivalry. It began when a replay official overruled a game official's penalty call on the field, thereby awarding the Packers a winning touchdown. Bears who played and fans who saw it live or on television still won't accept it.

The Bears had beaten the Packers eight straight times since 1985. Despite quarterback Don Majkowski's lost fumble and two interceptions, the Packers trailed only 13–7 when they took over at their own 27 with 4:44 left. "The Majik

Packers receiver Perry Kemp (81) catches a pass during what was dubbed the "instant replay game" in 1989 at Green Bay. The Packers won 14–13 after the disputed final play was reviewed by officials via instant replay—the refs ultimately decided in the Packers favor.

Man" got hot as he moved the chains to the Chicago 7-yard line on a variety of passes and runs, as well as smart clock management.

On the next play, the Bears sacked Majkowski at the Packers' 14-yard line. Two incomplete passes followed to set up fourth and goal. The Bears came at Majkowski with a heavy pass rush, which he evaded and ran toward the line of scrimmage. He rose, fired, and hit wide receiver Sterling Sharpe for an apparent touchdown with 32 seconds left as the Lambeau faithful erupted. Their cheers turned to jeers moments later when the crowd saw a flag on the field.

Line judge Jim Quirk had called a penalty on Majkowski, saying he threw the pass after he crossed the line of scrimmage. Upstairs, replay official Bill Parkinson checked the camera angles. To overturn Quirk's call, the replay had to offer conclusive proof he was wrong. Fans at home saw the play run over and over, and Chicagoans were certain they saw Majkowski's arm break the plane of the line of scrimmage before he threw.

After a long wait, a ruling came down, and the referee raised both arms to signal a touchdown. Chris Jacke kicked the extra point, and the Packers walked away with a 14–13 win that their fans always maintain was fair, just as Chicago fans to this day consider it highway robbery.

It was a call that so angered McCaskey that he ultimately led a successful move within the league to completely abolish instant replay in 1992. And it took until 1999 to get instant replay reinstated as an officiating tool, with the present referee-focused challenge system. Coincidentally, that was the same year Virginia McCaskey fired her son (making him the chairman of the board) and elevated Ted Phillips to the team presidency.

BILL SWERSKI AND DA BEARSSSS

Bill Swerski's Superfans was the brainchild of writer and actor Bob Smigel, originally created as *Chicago Superfans* for a 1988 improvisational comedy show performed in Chicago called *Happy, Happy, Good Show.* The skit depicted a television sports program where fans sit around a bar discussing the ongoing virtues of their favorite Chicago teams, predominantly the Bears.

Two Chicago radio hosts from the '70s and '80s inspired the skit. One was Bill Jauss, the longtime *Chicago Tribune* sportswriter and star panelist on WGN's *The Sportswriters,* and the other was WGN sportscaster Chuck Swirsky. Aptly named *Bill Swerski's Superfans,* the show portrayed a group of beer-swilling, sausage-stuffed superfans who discussed impending games and always predicted a Chicago victory in an exaggerated blue-collar dialect native to the Sout' or Sout'west Sides.

Smigel had moved on to NBC's *Saturday Night Live* as a writer when he convinced a producer to air the first *Bill Swerski's Superfans* sketch on January 12, 1991. The Superfans all wore dark sunglasses, Ditka-like moustaches, Bears clothing, and jeans. Most of the superfans were played by Chicago natives. Joe Mantegna played the original host Bill Swerski. The late Chris Farley played Todd O'Connor, who once predicted Da Bears would beat the New York Giants 79–0 because "Da Bears is like a wall. You can't go through it." Mike Myers played Pat Arnold, and Smigel was Carl Wollarski.

George Wendt became Bob Swerski, replacing Mantegna as Bill when he wasn't available—the explanation went that Bill "has had another heart attack." And after Myers left *SNL* for films, John Goodman became Pat Arnold with the explanation, "He has undergone a massive weight gain."

Set in Ditka's sports bar in River North in Chicago, they gorged themselves on ribs and sausages and swigged gallons of beer as they discussed Chicago sports. They hoisted fre-

Superfan Bob Swerski (played by George Wendt, right) introduces his nephew Bart Swerski (played by Horatio Sanz, middle) to Jimmy Fallon (left) on SNL's "Weekend Update" in 2003.

quent toasts to their heroes "Da Bearsss" and "Da Bullsss" with an occasional foray into baseball's Cubs and Sox. The Superfans appeared nine times between 1991 and 1997.

Their idol from the outset, and to this day in reincarnations of the sketch, is Ditka, "Da Coach." He made two *SNL* appearances in the sketch: once after Michael McCaskey fired him in 1993 and again in 1997 before Farley's death. In one of the more absurd conversations, the Superfans agreed that Ditka was so powerful that he could defeat a hurricane, until someone revealed that the hurricane was actually "Hurricane Ditka," a superstorm so powerful that it would win a competition for world dominance.

GAME DAY: THE '80s

For anyone who was there week after week, year after year, it truly is astonishing that the Chicago Bears of the 1980s won only a single Super Bowl. The late San Francisco 49ers coach and general manager Bill Walsh, an authority on sports in his own right, said many times that the Bears had the players and the goods to win at least three Vince Lombardi trophies, even perhaps as many as five. But that was contingent on good health and keeping the team together, neither of which happened.

After George Halas's death and the revival of the club under Mike Ditka, the Bears became the league's most popular team in terms of merchandise sales and the unquestioned leader in television ratings. Their overseas trip to London in 1986 for an August 3 exhibition game against—and ultimately a 17–6 victory over—the Dallas Cowboys at Wembley Stadium was a tour de force televised on NBC and given the royal treatment by *Sports Illustrated*.

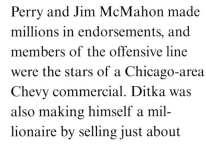

Da Coach! Mike Ditka–coached teams won 112 games, six NFC Central titles, appeared in three NFC championship games, and captured one Super Bowl in his 11-year tenure from 1982 to 1992.

William Perry and Jim McMahon made millions in endorsements, and members of the offensive line were the stars of a Chicago-area Chevy commercial. Ditka was also making himself a millionaire by selling just about

Jim McMahon and Walter Payton sign autographs in 1986 at the University of Wisconsin-Platteville during training camp.

everything, including the polar bears at Brookfield Zoo in an American Express spot.

For all the organization did to spruce up the old joint, Soldier Field remained an antiquated dowager. There were enough wooden supports buttressing the stands underneath the stadium to resemble an ancient European cathedral. The press box facilities were cramped and inadequate, and the plumbing often failed.

By the late '80s, the team had outgrown the original Halas Hall in Lake Forest. Plus, with the onset of free agency, the place became a hard sell to potential new Bears players who wanted the modern amenities that were commonplace with the other elite teams. Not having an indoor practice facility was the biggest problem. That became apparent when the team had to head as far south as Georgia when cold weather made practice outside in the elements in Lake Forest next to impossible. To their credit, the McCaskeys ultimately found the land to build a new, top-notch Halas Hall complex adjacent to the Tri-State Tollway.

Game day became an all-day event, much of it on Soldier Field's south parking lots. Serious tailgating took place, featuring drinks, cookouts, and plenty of lively fellowship before kickoffs and after the final gun, making each Bears game an event to remember. The Monsters of the Midway were the toast of the NFL both on and off the field, and this was still before *Saturday Night Live* debuted *Bill Swerski's Superfans* in 1991—an incredibly popular recurring skit paying homage to "Da Bears" and copious amounts of beer and Polish sausage.

A modern-day Bears pennant is a must for every fan.

This Mike Singletary figure is posed to play.

MIKE SINGLETARY

The *Chicago Tribune* paid tribute to Mike Ditka on January 15, 1993, after team president Michael McCaskey fired "Da Coach." Iron Mike exemplified the Halas credo: "Once a Bear, always a Bear."

This tabletop model displays the Old Soldier Field, as it looked before the 2002 remodeling project.

Ron Rivera played for the Chicago Bears from 1984 to 1992 and was a member of the Super Bowl XX team. He became the Bears defensive coordinator in 2006.

Buddy Ryan was the Bears' defensive coordinator in Super Bowl XX but left directly after to coach the Eagles.

The Bears' popularity had a wide reach—they were even featured on toy milk trucks.

IT LOOKED SO PROMISING

By 1990, the Bears had too many missing elements to rival the halcyon days of the middle '80s, but they remained formidable as long as Mike Ditka was still around to push, prod, goad, and lead them. After five straight NFC Central Division titles from 1984 to 1988, the wheels came off in late 1989.

The 1989 team opened with four impressive victories. However, they lost three straight—to Tampa Bay, Houston, and Cleveland—before they rebounded with a victory over the Rams. The instant replay game at Green Bay was tough to swallow but not the killer. That came three weeks later, when Joe Gibbs and the Redskins set a trap in Washington that ended in an overwhelming 38–14 rout and set off an irate Ditka in the locker room. After criticizing several players, including cornerback Donnell Woolford ("He can't cover anyone"), he cut loose with candor unlike anything anyone had ever heard, "We'll be lucky to win another game." He was right—they didn't.

To his credit, Ditka pulled himself and his team together in 1990; he might have done his best coaching that year. Jim Harbaugh took over at quarterback as Neal Anderson led the league's second-ranked ground attack with 1,076 yards and ten rushing touchdowns among his 13 total.

On defense, captain Mike Singletary was operating at his peak in the middle of a linebacking corps between Ron Rivera and Jim Morrissey and behind ends Richard Dent and Trace Armstrong, with a reliable rotation of Dan Hampton, William Perry, and Steve McMichael as veteran tackles. The key, though, was the play of the NFL Rookie of the Year, free safety Mark Carrier from USC, who led the league with ten interceptions.

The team went 9–1 to open the season before Minnesota routed them 41–13 on November 25; the Bears closed the regular season with four losses in their last six games. The NFC Central champions opened the playoffs at home with a 16–6 victory over Jim Finks's New Orleans Saints to set up their eighth postseason meeting with the New York Giants, this time at Giants Stadium in the New Jersey Meadowlands.

New York rolled to a 31–3 victory, more than making up for the two previous Ditka-coached victories over a Bill Parcells team. The Giants held Neal Anderson to 19 yards on 12 carries and fullback Brad Muster to eight yards on four attempts.

"I didn't think they would be able to beat us," said Mike Ditka. As Frank Litzky wrote in *The New York Times*, "He was so wrong."

Jim Harbaugh (4) is well-protected by center Jay Hilgenberg (63), guard Mark Bortz (62), and tackle Jimbo Covert (74) at Lambeau Field on September 16, 1990. The Bears beat the Packers 31–13.

END OF A DITKA DECADE

Rebounding from the playoff loss in the Meadowlands, the Bears opened the 1991 season with four straight wins. They capped the early streak with a 19–13 Monday night overtime win over the New York Jets. Tight end Cap Boso caught Jim Harbaugh's touchdown pass on the second-to-last play of the game. Unfortunately, instant replay determined that Boso was stopped just short of the goal line. Officials had to summon the players back onto the field (most were already in the locker rooms and out of their uniforms), and Jim Harbaugh snuck the ball in from one yard out for the final touchdown.

It became apparent in the next couple of weeks that Ditka's tenth Bears team was no longer operating in the league's upper echelon. The first indicator came in a visit to Buffalo, where overmatched rookie left tackle Stan Thomas jumped offsides three times in the first half. Marv Levy's AFC Super Bowl–bound Bills came alive in the second half to win easily, 35–20.

A week later, Joe Gibbs's Washington Redskins, who would represent the NFC in Super Bowl XXVI, manhandled the Bears 35–7. Not even a five-game winning streak, leaving the Bears at 9–2, could disguise the reality that the Chicago Bears were not a legitimate contender. It became even more obvious when Don Shula's underdog Miami Dolphins came to Chicago on a cold, late-November afternoon and stole a 16–13 overtime victory behind the accurate passes of Dan Marino.

Mike Ditka's Bears went 11–5 in his final season. It was a team with the thinnest talent since he became coach in 1982. Michael McCaskey fired him a year later.

Two weeks later, on December 8, 1991, the Bears beat the Packers 27–13 at Soldier Field, giving Ditka his 100th coaching victory. Only his mentor, George Halas, had won more games as a Bears coach. "When I came here, people said I wouldn't stay here," Ditka said. "I'm proud of the kind of football we have played for ten years."

Meanwhile, Jimmy Johnson and Jerry Jones had rebuilt their young and energetic Dallas Cowboys to open the playoffs at Soldier Field on December 29. Johnson and his rising young defensive coordinator Dave Wannstedt, a University of Pittsburgh alumnus like Ditka, had a solution for Ditka's power-football game. When the Bears got close to the Cowboys' end zone, Wannstedt's team went to a ten-man front: six linemen, four linebackers, and a lone defensive back.

Ditka did not counter with four wide receivers and short passes. Instead, he stubbornly stayed on the ground, and the Cowboys, who had built a 17–6 lead, stopped them three times in the red zone. The Bears managed a single touchdown to cut the deficit to 17–13. "Maybe we're a step away. Maybe we don't belong up there with the other teams," a battle-weary Ditka admitted. "Blame me."

His boss, Michael McCaskey, was doing just that. McCaskey was also taking notice of young Wannstedt's active, smart defensive schemes as well as the way Dallas handled the Bears in scoring territory.

CHAPTER FIVE

THE MODERN ERA
1993–TODAY

GAME 10
SEC 18 ROW 11 SEAT 28
239750-3

PACKERS
NOON SUNDAY • DEC 27, 1998
SOLDIER FIELD

"If we're going to win this thing, we're going to have to beat Green Bay twice."

GEORGE HALAS BEFORE THE 1963 CHAMPIONSHIP SEASON

Above: *The ticket for the Bears' season ender on December 27, 1998, honored Papa Bear. However, the team suffered a 13–10 loss to their ancient rivals from Green Bay.* **Right:** *Devin Hester has just broken into the clear on the way to giving the Bears a 7–0 lead on the opening kickoff at Dolphin Stadium in Miami for Super Bowl XLI on February 4, 2007. The Indianapolis Colts came back to win the Vince Lombardi Trophy 29–17.*

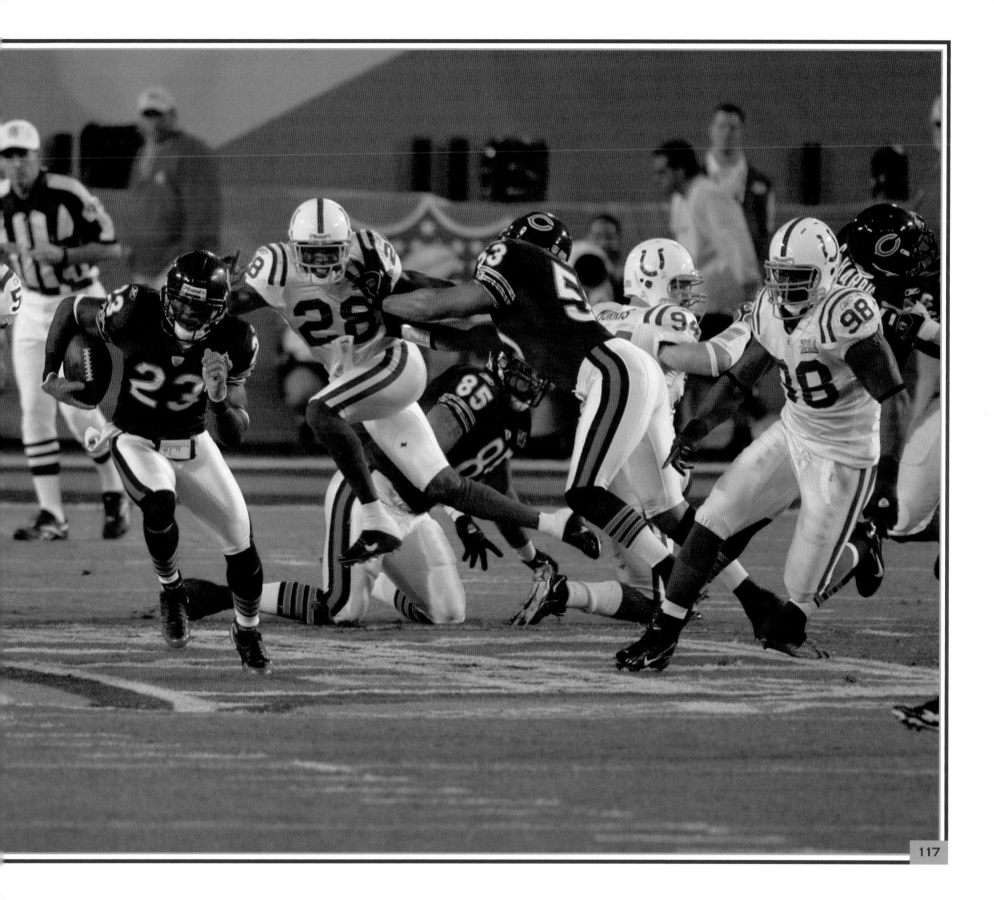

"BEAT GREEN BAY TWICE!"

George Halas's dictum has always been the mantra of the Chicago Bears, the representatives of the Illinois city that anchors the Midwest. Beating Chicago twice has always been the annual goal of the Green Bay Packers, the representatives of the Wisconsin industrial town 180 miles up the Lake Michigan shoreline. This passionate rivalry—the oldest sustained in the National Football League—is filled with more than just a little hate and plenty of nastiness.

These two teams are the winningest in the game: The Bears have won the most league games at 702; the Packers are second at 643. The Packers have won the most titles at 12; the Bears are second at 9. The Bears lead the 177-game series 91–80–6, and both teams' most famous coaches are the standards of excellence. Green Bay's Vince Lombardi, who masterminded five championships in seven years in the 1960s, is regarded as the best coach of all time. Chicago's George Halas won 324 league games and six titles, tying his greatest early rival, Packers founder Earl "Curly" Lambeau, for the most championships.

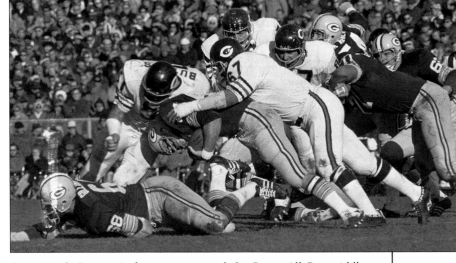

Green Bay's Donny Anderson is no match for Bears All-Pro middle linebacker Dick Butkus (51) and defensive tackle George Seals (67) on December 12, 1971, at Lambeau Field. The Packers won 31–10.

How great was Halas? Packers Hall of Famer Paul Hornung truly loved and honored Lombardi, his mentor, but he offered this perspective on the founder of Green Bay's greatest rival for *Papa Bear: The Life and Legacy of George Halas:* "Halas is the greatest name in the history of this game. No question. He is the father of professional football."

Halas was unquestionably the villain in the eyes of Packer fans, but he was respected for what he meant to Green Bay's NFL franchise. When other owners wanted out of there, Halas stood fast. And in 1956, he spearheaded a fundraising drive to build the modern 32,000-seat City Stadium, renamed Lambeau Field after the founder's death in 1965. It is fitting that the Packers opened their new stadium in 1957 against— who else?—the Bears, the heavily favored defending Western Conference champions. The Packers won 21–17.

The Bears play their first game against the Green Bay Packers in Green Bay at Bellevue Field in 1923. The second player from the left is Curly Lambeau, the founder and first coach of the Packers.

Both teams have hurt the other in major games through the years. The Packers knocked the Bears out of the 1968 playoffs in a 28–27 season closer at Wrigley Field. The Bears routed the Packers 35–7 in the home finale at Soldier Field in 2007, dealing with a –18 degree windchill factor that long-time nemesis Brett Favre called the worst playing conditions he ever had to endure.

Favre single-handedly dominated the series from 1992 to 2007, as Green Bay won 22 of the 32 Bears/Packers games. From 1994 to 2003, the Packers went 18–2, including the September 29, 2003, rededication of Soldier Field, when Favre threw three scoring passes in a 38–23 victory.

It's hard to imagine that the two teams faced each other just once in the postseason—in 1941, after they tied for the Western Division, both at 10–1. They played at Wrigley Field—

BEARS/PACKERS SHENANIGANS

The sideshow in the Bears/Packers rivalry belongs to the ardent fans who love their teams heart and soul. The closer to kickoff, the heartier the party gets and the more brats in Green Bay, hot dogs in Chicago, and beer in both places are consumed.

Fans are decked out in team colors and replica jerseys with headwear in blue and orange for Bear partisans and green and yellow for Packer backers—everything from early-season ballcaps to late-season skiwear. They shriek insults like children. "Packers suck!" yell Chicago fans. "Bears *still* suck!" counter the Green Bay loyalists.

No stunt has ever been more pungent than the 1985 game-day delivery of a five-pound bag of manure to the Bears locker room. It was sent from a Milwaukee radio station with a note that read, "Here's what you guys are full of." However, by the time the game was over, the Bears had fertilized Lambeau Field with pieces of the Packers and a 16–10 victory that sent the Bears on their way to Super Bowl XX.

This Bears fan expresses the sentiment of many of his fellow loyalists. It doesn't matter if they're in Chicago or Green Bay—Bears fans taunt the Packers whenever the National Football League's most enduring rivalry swings into high gear on game day.

Packers tight end Bubba Franks takes a hard hit from Bears linebacker Lance Briggs as he tries to make a reception in the December 4, 2005, game at Soldier Field. Franks had to leave the game after the play.

a week after Pearl Harbor was bombed—and the Bears hit the Packers with a 24-point second quarter thanks to the power running of Norm Standlee. The Bears took a 30–7 halftime lead on the way to a 33–14 triumph.

The last time both teams ranked top in the league was in 1963. The Bears won both games: 10–3 at Green Bay and 26–7 in the rematch at Wrigley Field on November 17. It was obviously the Bears' year after they beat the Giants 14–10 for the title. Vince Lombardi, who was in the stands, acknowledged, "I'm happy for Papa George. He's a helluva guy!"

REPLACING AN IDOL

After the 1992 season, Michael McCaskey took a vacation while Mike Ditka fretted in his office. When McCaskey returned on January 5, 1993, he called his grandfather's coaching choice into his office and fired him. In Chicago, Ditka was the most popular figure and McCaskey the most despised.

Thus, when McCaskey hired him, Dave Wannstedt had little chance to succeed with the fans. And it didn't help when it appeared that Wannstedt didn't know much about team traditions and rivalries, especially the rivalry that mattered most: Green Bay. In time, his personnel moves backfired and the players distrusted him.

Nonetheless, Wannstedt enjoyed a semblance of a honeymoon when the Bears reached the 1994 playoffs at 9–7 on the quarterbacking of Steve Walsh. Walsh then led them to a 35–18 wild-card win at Minnesota. Reality hit a week later in San Francisco, when the Super Bowl–bound 49ers routed the Bears 44–15.

After a 1995 season that saw the Bears finish at 9–7 on the right arm of Erik Kramer, McCaskey made linebacker Brian Cox the highest paid player in team history. He also re-signed Alonzo Spellman, the erratic defensive end, with a huge raise and let receiver Jeff Graham, Kramer's favorite target, go.

"All the pieces are in place," Wannstedt said about a potential Super Bowl run.

By the end of 1992, Michael McCaskey couldn't wait to get rid of Mike Ditka and hire Dallas assistant Dave Wannstedt. Wannstedt got the Bears to the playoffs in 1994, but his teams never went back. He left Halas Hall after the 1998 season with a disastrous 41–57 record.

Everything misfired in 1996. Kramer couldn't duplicate the statistical success he had enjoyed a season earlier, and journeyman addition Dave Kreig didn't do much better after taking over. Second-year running back Rashaan Salaam, the former Heisman Trophy winner who rushed for a team rookie record 1,074 yards the year before, fell flat on his face and would last only one more campaign in Chicago. The Bears finished a disappointing 7–9.

Before the 1997 draft, Wannstedt made the decision to trade the Bears' first-round, eleventh overall pick to Seattle for quarterback Rick Mirer and the Seahawks' fourth-round pick; Mirer flamed out and had to be cut. Back-to-back 4–12 seasons in 1997 and 1998 forced McCaskey to fire the man he brought to Chicago as the Bears' eleventh head coach. McCaskey's master plan had failed.

BUTTHEAD THE GREAT

For years, George Blanda led all Bears scorers with 541 points. That mark stood for 26 years, from 1958 until Bob Thomas passed him early in 1984 and ended with 629 points.

Kevin Butler, affectionately called Butthead by his teammates, joined the Bears in 1985. That same year, he set a one-season scoring record with 144 points. He was also successful on 31 of 38 field goal attempts and all 51 conversions. In the 1994 finale, Butler hit a field goal in a 13–3 loss at home to New England, giving him 1,002 career points. He added 114 more in 1995, finishing his career as the Bears' all-time scoring leader with 1,116 points. Walter Payton, with 125 touchdowns, is second with 750 points.

Butler drills an extra point against the Oilers at Soldier Field in 1989.

NO STARS, FEW WINS

The five seasons from 1994 to 1998—during Dave Wannstedt's tenure—were the most dismal in Bears history. After Mark Carrier, Richard Dent, and Donnell Woolford earned Pro Bowl slots in the 1993 season, Wannstedt failed to send a single Bear to Honolulu the rest of his time as head coach. Even during the team's playoff season in 1994, the Bears did not place a single player on the player-chosen NFC Pro Bowl squad.

It's not a coincidence that those Chicago Bears teams did not excel on the field. Their high watermarks under Wannstedt were 9–7 in both 1994 and 1995. The 1996 ("the pieces are in

In 1994, cornerback Donnell Woolford (25), defensive end Richard Dent (95), and safety Mark Carrier (20)—shown here in Honolulu—were the last Bears to play in a Pro Bowl game until 2000, when kick returner Glyn Milburn made the NFC squad.

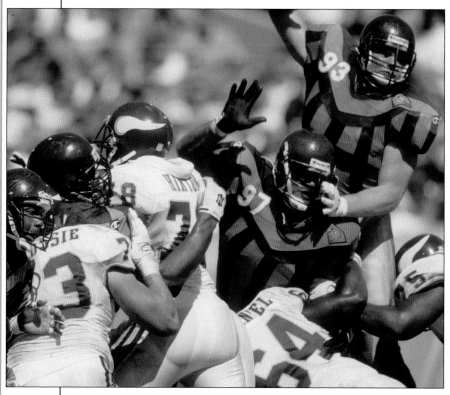

Times were tough in the Dave Wannstedt era as the Bears' records declined. Nothing seemed to work, not even the throwback uniforms; they sold as poorly as the team played.

place") team staggered to a 7–9 record before the 1997 and 1998 Bears fell to fifth and last in the NFC Central, ending both seasons with identical 4–12 records.

One of the few milestones during that period came in a 13–7 victory against the Tampa Bay Buccaneers on November 23, 1997, at Soldier Field: The Bears became the first National Football League franchise to reach the 600-victory mark. It was a mark that drew slight if not derisive interest from the Associated Press writer who covered the game. The lead read, "The Bears finally won a game at home, beating Tampa Bay with tough running from Raymont Harris and a defense that allowed only 35 yards rushing."

The Bucs got within a touchdown in the third quarter as Bears captain and linebacker Brian Cox got his second 15-yard penalty of the day for unsportsmanlike conduct when he shouted at officials after a Tampa Bay extra point. After the game, Cox announced he was quitting as team captain. "I don't want to go out for the coin toss," Cox said. "I don't want to have to look at the officials." The feeling was mutual.

This football has the signatures of all of the Bears' Pro Football Hall of Fame enshrinees.

Neal Anderson's Topps trading card shows him as a running back for the Bears. He ranks number two on Chicago's career rushing list with 6,166 yards.

This beer stein celebrates Soldier Field and its home-team players.

The *Daily Herald* northwest edition salutes Dick Jauron, the new Bears head coach, in 1999.

Leather football helmets were a part of the uniform from the 1920s to the 1940s. Modern-day Bears fans can purchase a replica of what Bears players wore during the glory days of football.

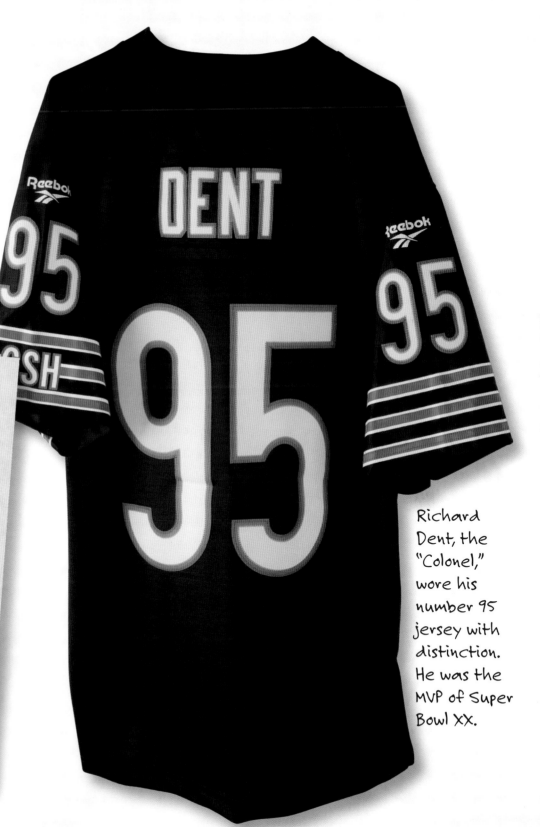

This program is from Walter Payton's induction to the Pro Football Hall of Fame in Canton, Ohio.

PRO FOOTBALL HALL OF FAME COLLECTION

Walter Payton
Induction Day – July 31, 1993

Richard Dent, the "Colonel," wore his number 95 jersey with distinction. He was the MVP of Super Bowl XX.

THE NEW HALAS HALL

The Bears moved into the 38-acre Halas Hall at Conway Park on March 3, 1997. Located just east of the Tri-State Tollway, the complex replaced the original Halas Hall on the campus of Lake Forest College, where the team had trained since 1979.

The new Halas Hall (shown on the Bears' 1997 Media Guide at left) is dedicated to the memory of the senior Halas, the team's founder, owner/president, and coach. It is a superb facility, built for the comfort of the large men who play pro football. The complex features a 100,000-square-foot office building, in contrast to the 32,000 square feet of the old Halas Hall. Inside are offices equipped to handle the operational and administrative staff, a 3,000-square-foot locker room with 62 lockers, and enough room to expand when the squad is at its training-camp maximum.

The team practices on two-and-a-half natural grass fields surrounded by a jogging path. The fields can drain up to nine inches of water per hour if needed, and grass grows into early winter because of heating elements under the fields.

For football players, the most attractive feature is the spacious weight room. Nearly four times larger than the cramped 1,800-square-foot facility in the old Halas Hall, this one is 7,000 square feet with as fine a setup as any in football. The east side of the weight room has a 28-foot-tall glass wall, providing a sense of spaciousness that helps the players with more productive workouts.

A 60-foot-long, two-lane lap pool is directly behind the weight room. The lanes have built-in resistance currents to stimulate sore and injured muscles. The training room is like a small clinic, with a doctor's office, X-ray facility, medical-records storeroom, casting room, whirlpool, cold-dip plunge, steam room, and sauna.

The team can get together in eight classrooms, two large meeting rooms, and a 150-seat auditorium, which is available for seminars, television productions, and news conferences.

Adjacent to the office building is a state-of-the-art indoor facility, the Walter Payton Center. Renovated in 2005, it's 400 feet long, 200 feet wide, and 85 feet high and has a synthetic football surface ringed by a two-lane running track.

For anyone who needs to get away for a bit of reflection, the Ed McCaskey Memorial Garden is situated immediately south of Halas Hall. It's a nicely landscaped cloverleaf-shape garden where trees, shrubs, and perennials are planted.

The Walter Payton Center is a state-of-the-art indoor practice space at the Halas Hall training facility in Lake Forest, Illinois. It holds a full-scale football field. At a height of 85 feet, the roof allows place kickers and punters to polish their skills.

JAURON GETS THE CALL

A 41–57 record and back-to-back 4–12 seasons did in Dave Wannstedt. At least Michael McCaskey waited until after Christmas before he fired him in 1998. And while the rest of the league gobbled up the prime coaching talent, McCaskey went skiing. By the time he returned, he still had one fortunate choice: Arizona Cardinals defensive coordinator Dave McGinnis, a popular and loyal assistant with Ditka and Wannstedt for 11 seasons. McGinnis was all set to hire Mike Martz, then at Washington, to run the offense.

After McCaskey made an offer on January 21, McGinnis asked to sleep on it. The next morning, the radio announced McGinnis as the new coach of the Bears. But there was a problem—he had not agreed to a contract. Figuring it was

Head coach Dick Jauron (left) was named NFL Coach of the Year for his 13–3 playoff season in 2001. Here, he accepts congratulations and a one-year contract extension from general manager Jerry Angelo at Halas Hall in January 2002.

McCASKEY OUT, PHILLIPS IN

After the McGinnis fiasco—the latest in a series of missteps—Michael McCaskey had become the laughingstock of the league. It took all Virginia McCaskey could muster to announce in public, on February 10, 1999, that she had fired her son Michael and was hiring family outsider Ted Phillips as president and chief executive officer.

Phillips originally joined the team's accounting department in 1983 and then became chief contract negotiator in 1987. He moved to vice president of operations in 1993. Phillips was made president and CEO mainly because he was the only person in the organization that Chicago Mayor Daley would talk to regarding a stadium deal—Daley had had many difficult go-rounds with McCaskey. Once Phillips took over, the movement toward a Soldier Field renovation proceeded smoothly.

a ploy to low-ball him, the furious McGinnis marched into Halas Hall and told the McCaskeys he could not work for them. By the time McGinnis and his wife got to O'Hare so they could head home, Dick Jauron was being introduced as the new coach.

The soft-spoken Jauron, one of the brightest stars in Yale's distinguished football history, played eight seasons as a well-regarded free safety at Detroit and Cincinnati. He had been an NFL assistant since 1985 and was defensive coordinator with the Jacksonville Jaguars when the Bears and fellow Yale alumnus McCaskey called.

Jauron was taking over a demoralized team. Every key position was a question mark, including middle linebacker, which was still waiting for a quality successor to Mike Singletary (retired since 1992). Fortunately for Jauron, the Bears had Olin Kreutz, who was drafted from Washington in the 1998 draft; he was a center in the worthy tradition of George Trafton, Bulldog Turner, Mike Pyle, and Jay Hilgenberg.

SWEETNESS SAYS GOODBYE

Chicago fans offered personal tributes to Payton at a public memorial service at Soldier Field on November 6, 1999.

On February 2, 1999, during a radio broadcast, Walter Payton announced that he had been diagnosed with a rare autoimmune disease called primary sclerosing cholangitis. The long-term disease causes scarring of the bile ducts and can also cause cancer, which it had in Payton. It had so aggressively attacked his liver, Walter said, that he needed an immediate transplant to survive.

At first there was hope, but by mid-spring the disease had advanced so quickly that a transplant was no longer feasible. All Sweetness, his family, friends, and thousands of fans could do was wait for the end. Payton's companions in his last days were his wife Connie, son Jarrett, daughter Brittany, and two of his closest friends from his Bears days, his South Barrington, Illinois, neighbor Mike Singletary and Matt Suhey, who became executor of his estate. Payton died at home on November 1, 1999, at only 45 years of age.

The Bears, who wore patches with the number 34 on their jerseys for the rest of the season (shown above right), held a public funeral service at Soldier Field. At the private service, John Madden, Governor George Ryan, Mayor Daley, as well as former teammates Suhey, Jim McMahon, Singletary, and Roland Harper joined the many mourners. The NFL also held special ceremonies at each game on November 7, 1999, to honor his career and considerable legacy.

That Sunday, Dick Jauron's Bears, struggling at 3–5, took Lambeau Field in Green Bay as decided underdogs, but they scratched, growled, and battled their way to a 14–13 victory over Brett Favre and the Packers when Bryan Robinson blocked Ryan Longwell's field goal attempt at the final gun. "I think Walter Payton picked me up, because I can't jump that high," Robinson said. "I just got my hand on that leather, and it felt so good. It's for you, Walter."

And the Walter Payton legacy continues. The Walter and Connie Payton Foundation stresses the need for organ donation, and the family also established the Walter Payton Cancer Fund in 2002—the same year Emmitt Smith broke Payton's career rushing record. The city of Chicago named Walter Payton College Prep high school in his honor. In 2007, the University of Illinois Medical Center opened the Walter Payton Liver Center; Chicago Metra commuters leaving Union Station see "#34 Sweetness" painted on a bridge piling at the south end of the yards.

Two athletic awards also honor Payton. The NCAA gives the Walter Payton Award to the best offensive player from Division 1 FCS (the old Division 1-AA), and the National Football League hands out the annual Walter Payton Man of the Year Award to players who excel in community service.

Above right: *The Bears painted Walter Payton's number 34 on their practice field in November 1999, after his death from liver cancer.* **Right:** *Bryan Robinson (98, top left) feels Walter Payton's spirit lift him as he deflects a short field goal attempt at Lambeau Field on November 7, 1999. The block gave the Bears a win that honored Payton, who had died the Monday before the game.*

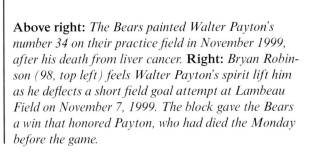

GM JERRY ANGELO

In Dick Jauron's second season, 2000, the Bears ranked near the bottom in every offensive category: 23rd in total yards, 21st in rushing yards, 23rd in passing yards, and 28th in total points, with 216 points against 355 for their opponents.

Jerry Angelo talks to the media at Halas Hall. He was named general manager on June 12, 2001, becoming the team's first GM since Jerry Vainisi was fired after the 1986 season. Counting Vainisi and Jim Finks, Angelo is only the third GM in team history.

Defense wasn't much better, ranking in or near the middle in every category. The only plus was rookie top-draft choice Brian Urlacher at middle linebacker, who justified his ninth overall selection by being named NFL Defensive Rookie of the Year.

The lone standout on offense was the steady but unspectacular play of third-year running back James Allen, who ran for 1,120 yards. Allen's longest gain of the season was just 29 yards. Curtis Enis suffered a knee injury in 1998; he was the second number-one running back to fail in the decade (the other was 1994 Heisman winner Rashaan Salaam who, like Enis, lasted three years).

The Bears' single bright spot in 2000 came with Jauron's second win at Green Bay, a 27–24 victory to open October. These Bears went 3–7 the rest of the way to finish at 5–11, fifth and last place in the NFC Central Division. It was clear that Jauron needed help.

After trying to function without a general manager since Vainisi in 1986, in a National Football League that featured free agency and salary caps among other basics, new CEO Ted Phillips took action. Smart enough to realize he was not a football man, let alone a general manager–type, he hired a consulting firm who recommended a career football man: Jerry Angelo.

Angelo, a Youngstown, Ohio, native, cut his football eyeteeth under the tutelage of Bo Schembechler at Miami University's "Cradle of Coaches," where he played defensive tackle from 1968 to 1970. He spent nine years as a college assistant before entering the pros in 1980 as a scout with Dallas. After stops in Calgary as a linebackers coach and with the New York Giants as a regional scout, he joined the Tampa Bay Bucs in 1987 as director of player personnel. When he joined Tampa Bay, the team averaged five wins a season. By the time he left for the Bears in 2001, Tampa Bay was building toward a victorious Super Bowl season in 2002.

Angelo's arrival came too late for the 2001 season. It was clear he had his own ideas on how to build a football team, and with the exceptions of Olin Kreutz and Urlacher, he did not like his personnel or his inherited coach.

This Larry, Moe, and Curly poster expressed the sentiment of many disgruntled fans who were unhappy with the 7–9 performance of a drab, uninspired team in 2003—the year the Bears returned to a rebuilt Soldier Field after a year's construction hiatus in Champaign, Illinois.

THE PLEASANT SURPRISE

The Bears figured to go nowhere in 2001. One noted expert, *Sports Illustrated*'s Paul Zimmerman, ranked the Bears at the bottom of the league. Neither Dr. Z nor Jerry Angelo counted on the coaching job Dick Jauron would deliver.

Jauron and ultraconservative offensive coordinator John Shoop got maximum mileage out of journeyman quarterback Jim Miller and Rookie of the Year running back Anthony Thomas. Thomas, from Michigan, came through with 1,183 yards and 7 touchdowns among the 37 touchdowns the team scored all season.

Back-to-back, almost-impossible, come-from-behind over-time victories in midseason propelled the Bears into control of the Central Division. Trailing 28–9 in the fourth quarter against the San Francisco 49ers at Soldier Field on October 28, 2001, Shane Matthews, in relief of the injured Miller, con-nected for a pair of touchdowns with rookie David Terrell. Then Thomas scored the two-point conversion to set up over-time. On the first overtime play, Jeff Garcia's pass bounced

James Allen catches Shane Matthews's heave with assistance from David Terrell (83), Marty Booker (86), and Dez White (80) at 00:00 of regulation time to shatter the Cleveland Browns and force overtime at Soldier Field on November 4, 2001. The Bears won 27–21 on Mike Brown's interception return.

JAURON: 2001 COACH OF THE YEAR

Nobody better deserved the honor of NFL Coach of the Year than the Bears' Dick Jauron for what he accomplished in 2001. Jauron was the third Bears coach—after George Halas and Mike Ditka—to win 13 games in one season and third to be named Coach of the Year. Halas won the honor twice, in 1963 and 1965; Ditka won it in 1985 and 1988.

The 2001 season was the first time the Bears had won the NFC Central outright since 1990, and with realignment set for 2002, the Bears were the last NFC Central champion. "Any individual awards are flatter-ing, but I'd accept them for the football players and staff first and foremost as well as the whole organization," Jauron told *Bear Report,* the Chicago magazine dedicated to Bears coverage.

off Terrell Owens's shoulder pads and into strong safety Mike Brown's hands. He ran it back 33 yards for the winner. "This is unbelievable," Brown said.

That was mere prelude to the following week. Trailing 21–7, Matthews connected with Marty Booker to make it 21–14 with 28 seconds left. After recovering an onside kick, Matthews fired a Hail Mary to the end zone and James Allen grabbed it in a scramble to force overtime. Then, on the third play of overtime, Bryan Robinson tipped a Tim Couch pass and Mike Brown again intercepted, scoring from 16 yards out. This time he ran all the way out of the stadium. There was nothing else to say.

Snow was falling as the Bears beat the Jacksonville Jaguars 33–13 to finish their remarkable regular season at 13–3. They then drew a bye week in the playoffs. Nobody was talking 1985 yet, but more than a few thought about it.

JANUARY 2002: THE PARTY'S OVER

The bulldozers were lined up ominously, waiting for the finish of the Bears/Eagles playoff game that afternoon so they could begin the demolition of the old Soldier Field. Unfortunately for the Bears, the Eagles came armed and ready to end it all as mercilessly as a hangman kicking the footstool out from underneath his victim.

The realistic end for the 2001 Bears came early. With the Eagles up 6–0 on a pair of field goals, Philly's Damon Moore intercepted Jim Miller's third-down pass in the end zone and ran it back to his own 20. Meanwhile, defensive end Hugh Douglas picked Miller up and slammed him to the ground. The referee did not penalize Douglas even though 15 years earlier at Soldier Field, Green Bay's Charles Martin was tossed out after he dumped Jim McMahon on his shoulder to end his season. Douglas's deed finished Miller's season with a separated right shoulder.

"It was a shame," Miller's replacement Shane Matthews said, along with the fighting words, "a cheap shot."

"He was fair game," Douglas retorted. Several Bears tried to retaliate, but Douglas kept his head on a swivel, took some shots, and survived the rest of the game. Without Miller, "The team's offense" as Dave Anderson wrote in *The New York Times,* "appeared lost."

The Bears didn't go down easily, however. They took a 7–6 lead on Ahmad Merrit's 47-yard reverse before the Eagles got ahead 13–7 with native Chicagoan Donovan McNabb's scoring pass to his fellow Chicago-area teammate, Evanston's Cecil Martin. Jerry Azumah's early third-quarter interception and subsequent 39-yard runback gave the Bears their final 14–13 lead.

Then McNabb took over. He led the Eagles with 262 yards passing and finished with a 37-yard touchdown run to wrap up the 33–19 win. "It's a disappointing end to a very good season," coach Dick Jauron said afterward. "The loss is very disappointing to all of us. We believe we can beat anybody."

Those still left out of the crowd of 66,944 who packed the colonnaded lakefront stadium exited quickly and quietly after the final gun. The big bulldozers and the crane swinging the wrecking ball took over the noisemaking on this new construction site that would see its next football game on the last Monday of September 2003.

Ahmad Merritt (81) dives into the end zone at the end of a 47-yard touchdown run for a 7–6 Bears lead in their playoff game with Philadelphia at Soldier Field on January 19, 2002. The Eagles won the final game at the old Soldier Field 33–19.

Even Mr. Potato Head is a loyal fan of the Chicago Bears.

Pro Football Weekly honors quarterbacks Sid Luckman and Erik Kramer in the '94 season as a celebration of the Bears' diamond Jubilee.

This pennant proudly supports pro football's founding franchise.

The rivalry continues: Packers fans have their cheeseheads; Chicago Bears fans retaliate with a foam Bears head.

Olin Kruetz
Center

Kids Club

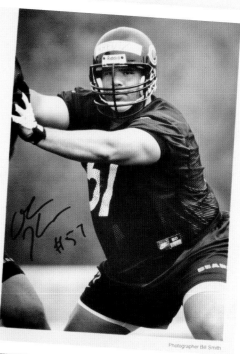

#57

Photographer Bill Smith

Top NFL center Olin Kreutz signed this practice photo. He earned six Pro Bowl slots in 11 seasons from 1999 to 2008.

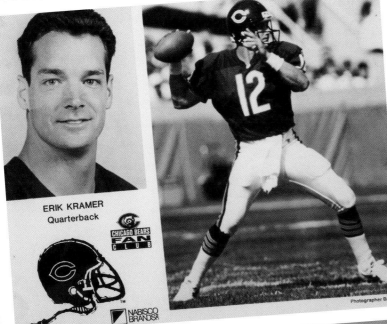

ERIK KRAMER
Quarterback

CHICAGO BEARS FAN CLUB

NABISCO BRANDS

Photographer Bill Smith

Erik Kramer is getting ready to pass in this fan club giveaway. He had 3,838 passing yards and 29 touchdown passes in 1995.

#1 FAN

When Chicago Bears fans put on this foam finger, there is no doubt what it means.

BRIAN URLACHER

No National Football League team has turned out such an outstanding succession of superstar linebackers as the Chicago Bears. The tradition that started with George Trafton in 1920 and was continued by Clyde "Bulldog" Turner, as well as outside linebacker George Connor, gained new meaning in 1953, when middle guard Bill George took up his stance behind the line and invented the middle linebacker position. The legendary Dick Butkus followed George, and then Mike Singletary refined the position. When Brian Urlacher joined the Bears in 2000, he brought a whole new dimension to the position, becoming Defensive Rookie of the Year.

Urlacher, who has played most of his pro career at a solid 6′4″, 258 pounds, is a unique athlete. He is exceptionally strong and powerful, and he is gifted not only with superior speed, but also quickness, and an ability to cover sideline-to-sideline then drop back 25 to 30 yards if necessary. He is a hard hitter and a sure tackler, and he has become a modern model for a middle linebacker, on the same level with the Baltimore Ravens' Ray Lewis. Back and neck trouble have slowed him down, but Urlacher remained a powerful force in 2008, his ninth season with the Bears.

Brian Urlacher takes off in pursuit of the opposing team. He is one of the NFL's most productive linebackers and has been to the Pro Bowl six times.

Urlacher was all-state wide receiver and safety at Lovington High School in New Mexico. He played outside linebacker, free safety, and wide receiver at the University of New Mexico before Mark Hatley drafted him with the ninth overall pick in 2000. He was voted to the AP All-Pro team after the 2001, 2002, 2005, and 2006 seasons and named to six NFC Pro Bowl teams from 2000 to 2003 and in 2005 and 2006.

The Bears hold Urlacher in high regard—in 2003 they signed him to a nine-year contract that runs through 2011 (it was renegotiated with a substantial raise before the 2008 season). Urlacher has made at least 100 tackles a season for nine consecutive seasons through 2008. In 2002 alone, he made 214 tackles. In 2005, he was named the NFL's Defensive Player of the Year; the only other Bear to win that award was Mike Singletary, who earned it twice.

Urlacher is a national fan favorite. His Bears jersey, number 54, has ranked at or near the top of NFL jersey sales, along with Brett Favre's number 4.

In 2002, Urlacher appeared on *Wheel of Fortune* and won more than $47,000, which he donated to charity. He has also been a supporter and fundraiser for the Special Olympics and Ronald McDonald House.

THE LONG, HOMELESS SEASON

The Bears entered the 2002 season with high hopes of replicating the magical 2001 campaign that closed out the old Soldier Field. The Bears were confident that they would thrive in the loud Memorial Stadium in Champaign, Illinois, before friendly crowds of season-ticket holders from Chicago, central Illinoisans, and local college students.

The Illini's playing surface, a gridiron of woven plastic grass on top of ground rubber pebbled from auto tires, became a 108-degree griddle as the Bears opened against Minnesota. Huge defensive tackles Ted Washington and Keith Traylor, who so effectively clogged the middle in 2001, practically collapsed in the stifling conditions. Defensive end Philip Daniels blamed the surface for a knee sprain. With Chicago trailing 23–20, Mike Brown intercepted Daunte Culpepper, setting up Jim Miller's drive and winning touchdown pass to David Terrell, giving the Bears a 27–23 win.

Two weeks later, the Bears returned to Champaign and opened a 20–0 lead on New Orleans before a series of mistakes resulted in a 29–23 loss. That launched a dismal eight-game losing streak tied for the worst in team history with the eight-game losing streak of 1978. Two losses in that streak came on Monday nights—the first against the Packers, when the Bears wore all navy blue for the first time and laid a huge egg on national television in a Brett Favre–driven 34–21 defeat. Five weeks later, Marc Bulger picked apart the Bears secondary for 347 yards in a 21–16 St. Louis Rams win. That came a week after Tom Brady rallied the New England Patriots from a 27–6 third-quarter deficit to a 33–30 win.

In 2002, the Bears played their home games at Memorial Stadium in Champaign, Illinois, while Soldier Field was being renovated. The Eagles won this game 19–13.

The Bears finally reversed their course at Memorial Stadium on November 24 against Detroit. Miller, who had been out with a bad elbow, came on to lead the Bears to ten points in the closing three minutes. Paul Edinger's 22-yard field goal forced overtime as time ran out. The Bears got in position for Edinger to kick a 40-yard field goal to win it. Lions coach Marty Mornhinweg left everyone scratching their heads with his reasoning, "Knowing the outcome of this game, I wouldn't do it again. But in a similar situation, I would."

The Bears finished the season with a 15–0 loss to eventual Super Bowl champion Tampa Bay. The Bears were ready to leave the prairie and return to sweet home Chicago.

The Bears play their first home game outside Chicago since 1920 at Memorial Stadium in Champaign on August 10, 2002. The Denver Broncos won the exhibition opener 27–3, which was just the beginning. The Bears ended with a disappointing 4–12 season coming off the playoffs in 2001.

133

AN OLD FACE ON A NEW BODY

*T*he New York Times critic Herbert Muschamp, an admitted modernist, loved the way architects Ben Wood (of Chicago) and Carlos Zapata had "liberated" sports architecture with a design he called "easily a match for the most advanced stadium design in the world."

Pulitzer Prize–winning *Chicago Tribune* architectural critic Blair Kamin did not approve of the design; he described the new stands as heavily weighing down the "once-proud" columns, as if "Super Bowl hero William 'Refrigerator' Perry had plunked down his ample haunches on a picket fence." Furthermore, Kamin called the new field a "big poke in the eye" and its placement on the lakefront "inexcusable."

The new Soldier Field became an art museum of sorts, in keeping with its anchor position on Chicago's Museum Campus, which includes the Field Museum of Natural History, Shedd Aquarium, and Adler Planetarium. The Memorial Water Wall, which leads from the north parking garage and entrance to the stadium, is a 280-foot-long wall of polished granite with eight medallions honoring the different branches of the armed forces. Water continuously flows over the sculptured memorial. It is the only marker open year-round to non-paying customers.

Other markers include the Ring of Honor on the mezzanine level that commemorates each of the 26 Bears Hall of Famers; the Bears Den, a walkthrough of Bears history on the

The old plastic seats have been torn out and discarded as scrap as construction crews begin the Soldier Field renovation in January 2002. The renovation took a year and a half and forced the team to play its 2002 home games at Memorial Stadium in Champaign, Illinois.

lower concourse of the west grandstands; and the Doughboy Statue, which honors the fighting men of World War I and is situated on the Grand Concourse just inside the Gate O south entrance. Originally dedicated and located in Garfield Park in the 1930s, it was severely damaged before being beautifully restored and rededicated in Soldier Field.

Farther along the main concourse on the west side is the display that honors the memory of George Halas. It demonstrates his remarkable energy, and in bas-relief and laser images, it depicts his eras, including the founding, the 73–0 title victory in Washington, a Wrigley Field crowd, Halas with his son, and Bears greats such as Red Grange, Dick Butkus, and Walter Payton. For some unexplained reason, Mike Ditka's image is not included. Unfortunately, this memorial cannot be seen by the general public.

Michael McCaskey said he was proud of the new stadium. However, he did acknowledge that "we need victories."

Chicago mayor Richard M. Daley inspects the scale model of the "new" Soldier Field. After the 19-month renovation was completed, the stadium seated more than 61,000 fans.

The grand re-opening of Soldier Field was held Monday night, September 29, 2003, starring the Bears and Green Bay Packers. Scores of former players came, including many who had played for coach Mike Ditka. Ditka did not attend but gave a taped introduction to the fans, who watched it on the video boards located at each end of the stadium. Several of Ditka's teammates on George Halas's 1963 championship team were also in attendance.

Dan Hampton, the newest Hall of Fame inductee, addressed the crowd live at halftime. Mike Singletary, then an assistant coach in Baltimore, even flew in for the event. Unfortunately, the Packers spoiled the party, dealing the Bears their third straight loss of the young season, 38–23. Luckily, there would be other games at the new Soldier Field with more favorable and memorable outcomes.

It's back to business for the Bears in their second game at the newly renovated Soldier Field on October 5, 2003. The Bears took on the Oakland Raiders, beating them 24–21.

SOLDIER FIELD BY THE NUMBERS

Capacity in the reconstructed Soldier Field is 61,500 individual seats. For $655 million, Chicago and the National Football League got a massive facility with underground garages for 4,400 vehicles; parking for 3,100 more in the tailgate-friendly south lot between the stadium and McCormick Place; seating tiers that stretch as high as 151 feet on the west side; and luxury boxes, with an array of amenities, behind green-tinted glass atop the east side.

Whereas 60 percent of the seats in the old Soldier Field bowl were situated behind the goal lines, 60 percent of the seats in the new configuration fall within the goal lines. Each seat, with the fan in mind, directly faces the field. Sightlines from every seat are superior—as fine as any in the league. Virtually all the seats that face north give fans the same view of Chicago's marvelous downtown skyline that viewers across America enjoy each time they see a Bears game on television.

THE NAME IS LOVIE

Dick Jauron's five-year tenure ended at the conclusion of the 7–9 2003 season. General manager Jerry Angelo went after his longtime friend, LSU coach Nick Saban, but the deal collapsed. It was speculated that Saban had demanded personnel control and that Angelo would not cede.

Angelo finally turned to the NFL, and on January 15, 2004, he introduced St. Louis Rams defensive coordinator Lovie Smith as the team's 13th head coach and its first African American to hold the job. Angelo (then the personnel director at Tampa Bay) met Smith when Tony Dungy hired him to coach the linebackers for the Buccaneers. The quiet Smith absorbed Dungy's Cover 2 defense and took it to his next two stops: as defensive coordinator for the Rams and as head coach in Chicago.

Smith told the media that he intended to augment a basic, three-point plan: Beat Green Bay and end the Packers' dominance of the NFC North Division; win the division; and win the Super Bowl. Within three years, Smith's Bears would accomplish the first two goals, and they would reach the NFL championship game.

Smith said he wanted to run an attacking defense, stressing takeaways, thus he imported Chicago favorite Ron Rivera

During the NFC divisional playoff at Soldier Field on January 15, 2006, head coach Lovie Smith (with defensive assistants) talks tactics with (left to right) Lance Briggs, Charles Tillman, and Adewale Ogunleye (93).

from Philadelphia as defensive coordinator. At Angelo's insistence, he brought in Dick Vermeil's quarterbacks coach in Kansas City, Terry Shea, and made him offensive coordinator. It turned out to be a disaster that earned Shea his walking papers.

Smith ordered linemen to shed pounds and start running; he wanted a lean, fast, tough team, able to operate in his gap-coverage defense.

After losing the 2004 opener to the Lions at home, the Bears went to Green Bay and came away with a 21–10 win. Rex Grossman put the Bears up 7–3 on an 11-yard touchdown pass to fullback Bryan Johnson. Then, the Packers were at the Bears' 2-yard line just before halftime when Brian Urlacher stripped the ball from Ahmad Green. Mike Brown picked it up and raced 95 yards to score—it was his fifth career defensive touchdown. The superb play was dampened late in the game when Brown left with a torn Achilles tendon. The Bears also lost cornerback Charles Tillman to a knee injury.

"I've never been in a fight where some guy told me he was going to beat me up, and he beat me up," Packers linebacker Nick Barnett said of the Bears that day.

A week later at Minnesota, Grossman went down with a torn knee ligament. Still, the future looked brighter.

21ST CENTURY GAME DAY

The Bears charge out of the northwest tunnel to take the home field, led by Staley Da Bear—their mascot since they returned to a remodeled Soldier Field in 2003.

Like other professional sporting events, attending a game has turned into a major production each week during football season. The Bears have drastically changed the way they present a ballgame, doing their best to make it a total experience for fans young and old, from well before kickoff to well after the final snap.

By the turn of the 21st century, the days of marching bands, halftime Pop Warner football games, and the Honey Bears were gone. Live music was replaced by canned music, with sound effects and organized cheers integrated into a huge video board display.

Just before kickoff, fans watch the team emerge through the jaws of an inflated orange and blue bear head. When the cannon booms, flag bearers—along with Staley Da Bear—lead the team out through smoke in a dash toward center field while the public address system blares a semi-rock version of "Bear Down, Chicago Bears." The fans respond—if they are actually attentive to what is happening on the field. It's not hard to get distracted with all the extra razzle-dazzle that wasn't present back in the old days.

Besides the organized activity, there is plenty going on at Soldier Field. Tailgating remains a major outdoor sport in good weather and bad, and the game itself is still the best show in town. Before the 1998 season, however, the Bears announced that there would be no tailgating in the lots while the game was being played. The pregame experience had got-

ten so big that many of the participants showed up for the tailgating alone—they watched the game from the parking lot on televisions plugged into generators. The new edict curtailed such festivities—anyone in the lots during the game had to leave.

Inside the stadium, huge message boards feature replays, highlights, statistics, quizzes, historic footage, and when time allows, out-of-town highlights.

It's tailgate time outside Soldier Field. The good times roll before fans get down to the business of watching football.

No fan who attends a game at Soldier Field should be able to say there was no information available!

STALEY DA BEAR

In 2003, the Bears did away with the "Bear Man" character and introduced a furry mascot they call Staley Da Bear. Wearing a Bears jersey over his furry top, Staley, named for the previous team nickname of 1920 and 1921, wears uniform number 00 and sets about his mission to entertain young and old.

The Bears also use Staley for a variety of events and charities. They hold an annual Run with Staley one-mile children's race at their training camp on the campus of Olivet Nazarene College in Bourbonnais, Illinois. Each child gets a T-shirt and a medal of participation.

Additionally, the Bears have made Staley available for schools in conjunction with the NFL's First and Goal program. He promotes health in a high-energy show. Staley also participates in all-school pep rallies including "Back to School Kick Off," "Tackle Reading," and "How to Handle that ISAT (Illinois Standards Achievement Test)."

STEPPING UP TO THE PLAYOFFS

What a difference a year would make! In 2005, quarterback Rex Grossman would be out for the first 13 weeks after he suffered a broken ankle in an August exhibition game at St. Louis. New offensive coordinator Ron Turner, who was in his second tour with the Bears after an eight-year stretch as head coach at Illinois, turned to rookie Kyle Orton from Purdue. Turner kept a tight leash on Orton, who was just learning the ropes. Turner made him play as a disciplined "game manager" instead of a gunslinger. And fortunately, Orton responded.

After a shaky 9–7 opening-game loss at Washington, the Bears showed promise in the home opener in Week 2, when Thomas Jones's 139 rushing yards led to a 38–6 victory over the outgunned Detroit Lions. After Chicago lost back-to-back games to AFC Central teams Cincinnati and Cleveland, Bear fans were concerned. But Orton threw a pair of touchdown passes to tight end Desmond Clark as the Bears easily handled the Vikings 28–3.

They were at 9–3 when they went to Pittsburgh on December 11 but were overpowered in the snow by the Super Bowl–bound Steelers 21–9. A week later, they were hanging on to a 6–3 lead over Atlanta on a cold Sunday night when Grossman came off the bench in his first appearance of the season. He sparked the team to a 16–3 victory and led the Bears to a division-clinching 24–17 win at Green Bay a week later.

Playoffs dominated local conversation from Christmas to the January 15, 2006, divisional playoff at Soldier Field against the Carolina Panthers. The Bears had looked strong in late November when they beat the Panthers 13–3. This time, though, they could not stop the lethal combination of quarterback Jake Delhomme and wide receiver Steve Smith; those two showed their stuff on the second play of the game, a 58-yard scoring pass that resulted from Charles Tillman's loss of footing. Smith's athletic, acrobatic big plays bedeviled the Bears all afternoon. When the Bears closed to 16–14, Smith faked cornerback Chris Thompson and caught an easy 39-yard scoring pass. He made 12 catches for 218 of Delhomme's 319 passing yards in a 29–21 Carolina win.

Coach Lovie Smith admitted the Bears had failed to prevent Smith from making big plays. "We were unable to do that," he said.

When asked what happened, Brian Urlacher said, "Steve Smith is what happened to us. He just kept making plays. He is the best offensive player in the league."

Nathan Vasher (31), Tank Johnson (99), and Adewale Ogunleye (93) apply the gang-tackle sandwich to an unfortunate Minnesota running back at Soldier Field on October 16, 2005. The Bears won 28–3.

THE RIDICULOUS DEVIN HESTER

By the time Bears radio announcer Jeff Joniak blurted out, "Devin Hester, you are ridiculous!" the speedster from Riviera Beach, Florida, and the University of Miami had become—hands down—the most electrifying player in the National Football League.

Nobody had burst onto the big stage in Chicago with such an impact since Gale Sayers in 1965. Hester was an unstoppable blur and, like Sayers, a scoring threat at any time, from any point on the field, when he got his hands on the ball.

Hester came to the Bears as the 57th selection in the 2006 draft—a second-rounder. He had no position; he hoped to play defensive back and thought the coaches might also try him at wide receiver. When they saw him return kicks, the Bears knew precisely what kind of gem they possessed.

Hester had run back long punts against both Green Bay and Arizona before the Bears took on the New York Giants on *NBC Sunday Night Football*. A Giants field goal attempt sailed near the back of the end zone, where Hester caught it and took a couple of casual forward steps. And then he turned it on. He cut to the right sideline and took off all the way—108 yards for a touchdown to tie the league record that

Devin Hester breaks free to return this punt for the winning touchdown at the University of Phoenix Stadium in Glendale, Arizona, on October 16, 2006. The Bears beat the Cardinals 24–23 in an incredible Monday night comeback.

teammate Nathan Vasher had set a year earlier against the 49ers. Another punt-return touchdown against Minnesota preceded three kickoff runbacks. Then he opened Super Bowl XLI with a 92-yard dandy, giving the Bears a lead they could not hold.

Hester ran back four punts and two kickoffs in 2007 to give him a dozen career returns for scores in regular-season play, as well as one in the Super Bowl. All-Pro honors and Pro Bowl appearances followed both the 2006 and 2007 seasons. By that time in his career, Hester was being called the greatest kick returner in history. In 2008, he had no runbacks for touchdowns—he concentrated on the wide receiver position.

"He's still a very young receiver," offensive coordinator Ron Turner told the *Chicago Sun-Times*. "At some point it starts to click." For Hester, it has always seemed to click.

A SUPER BOWL FIRST

The Colts' Adam Vinatieri kicked off to the Chicago 8-yard line, and Devin Hester caught it near the corner to open Super Bowl XVI at Dolphin Stadium. Then every kid's highlight fantasy began: Hester ran to the middle, froze for an instant at the 25 to set up the play, and shot forward. He dashed to his right and had only Vinatieri to beat—which he did. A mere 14 seconds had elapsed when Hester reached the end zone, becoming the first player to open a Super Bowl with a touchdown runback.

"It was a great show at the time," Hester said after the Bears lost 29–17. "They won't remember the return. They'll remember the team that won."

George Halas was honored in 1997, when the United States Postal Service issued a 32-cent stamp with his likeness in Chicago on August 16.

This fur hat guarantees a warm head for any fan in the coldest Bear weather.

A Bears garden gnome will protect a hardcore fan's precious plants.

The Bears' 600th victory, on November 23, 1997, was commemorated with a pin. It was a 13-7 win over the Tampa Bay Bucs at Soldier Field.

Walter Payton's 1920s throwback jersey was issued as part of the NFL's 75th anniversary celebration in 1994.

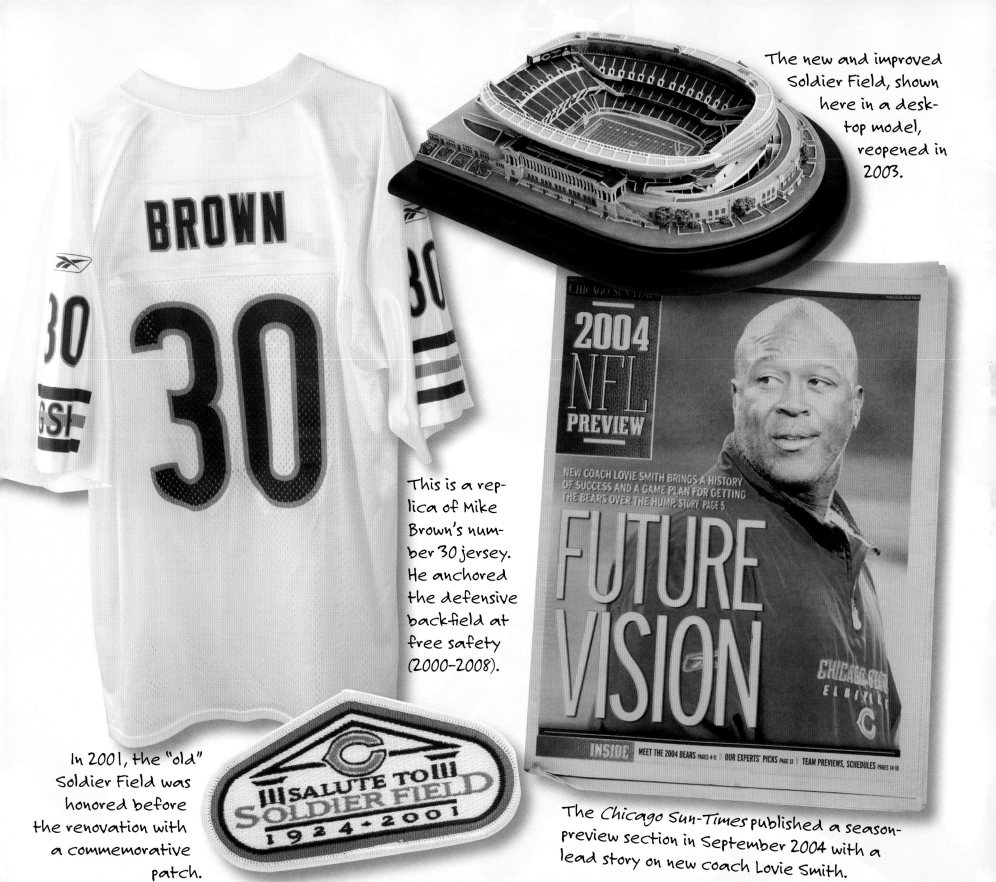

The new and improved Soldier Field, shown here in a desk-top model, reopened in 2003.

This is a replica of Mike Brown's number 30 jersey. He anchored the defensive backfield at free safety (2000–2008).

NEW COACH LOVIE SMITH BRINGS A HISTORY OF SUCCESS AND A GAME PLAN FOR GETTING THE BEARS OVER THE HUMP. STORY, PAGE 5.

2004 NFL PREVIEW

FUTURE VISION

INSIDE   MEET THE 2004 BEARS PAGES 4-11 ‖ OUR EXPERTS' PICKS PAGE 13 ‖ TEAM PREVIEWS, SCHEDULES PAGES 14-18

In 2001, the "old" Soldier Field was honored before the renovation with a commemorative patch.

‖SALUTE TO‖ SOLDIER FIELD 1924·2001

The Chicago Sun-Times published a season-preview section in September 2004 with a lead story on new coach Lovie Smith.

RETURN TO THE SUPER BOWL

The Bears had two goals in mind as they opened the 2006 season: reaching and winning the Super Bowl. They showed their determination as they roared out of the gate with seven impressive victories, opening with a 26–0 shutout at Green Bay led by the lockdown defense and Rex Grossman's quarterbacking. Devin Hester's 84-yard punt return served notice that the Bears could score at any time, from any place.

They had only two close calls in those first seven games. One was a tough 19–16 win over the Vikings in the din of the Hubert Humphrey Metrodome. Another was a bit of Monday night madness in the Cardinals' new University of Phoenix Stadium, where they overcame a 23–3 deficit to win 24–23, a victory that left Arizona coach Dennis Green sputtering in frustration. "We let them off the hook," was Green's mildest comment in his expletive-filled postgame press conference.

In his worst effort of the season, Grossman threw four interceptions and lost two fumbles, and he had a problem hitting receivers. Those troubles were magnified two weeks later when the Miami Dolphins, led by linebacker Jason Taylor, took over Soldier Field in a 31–13 rout. Grossman still had issues the following Sunday night in New York but connected on a late first-half touchdown pass to Mark Bradley as the Bears came alive to beat the Giants 38–20.

Two weeks later, after beating the Jets in the Meadowlands, the Bears went to New England, where Tom Brady led the Patriots to their hard-fought 17–13 win. After that, the only tough test to sew up home-field advantage came at Soldier Field, where the Tampa Bay Buccaneers took the Bears to

Chris Harris (46) and Brian Urlacher (54) attack Colts running back Joseph Addai in the first quarter of Super Bowl XLI in Miami on February 4, 2007.

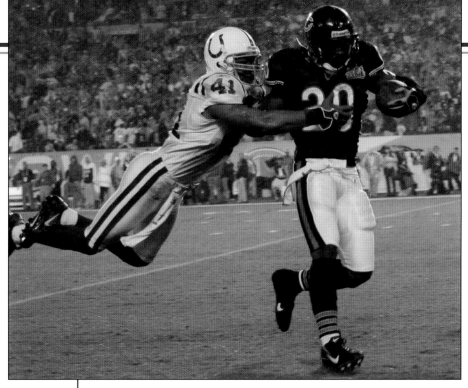

Colts safety Antoine Bethea brings down Bears running back Thomas Jones during a 52-yard rushing play in Super Bowl XLI at Dolphin Stadium in Miami.

overtime before Robbie Gould drilled a sudden-death field goal for a 34–31 victory.

As smoothly as things had gone, the Bears were operating without defensive tackle Tank Johnson, who became a major off-the-field distraction for the team. While he was on probation for an earlier weapons violation, Johnson's trouble worsened on December 14, 2006, when Gurnee, Illinois, police went to his home and confiscated six weapons, including two assault rifles. A few days later, Johnson was at the Ice Bar in Chicago's River North area when his best friend and bodyguard William Posey was killed in a fight on the dance floor. Johnson was ordered to home confinement and had to get permission from league commissioner Roger Goodell to travel with the Bears to the Super Bowl.

Getting there wasn't easy. The Seattle Seahawks, a team the Bears beat 37–6 in October, were their first playoff opponent. Behind Shaun Alexander's 108 yards, Seattle led 24–21 in the third quarter. Grossman brought the Bears back, allowing Gould to send them into overtime on a 41-yard field goal.

In sudden death, Grossman hit Rashied Davis on a 30-yard pass play. Almost five minutes into overtime, Gould calmly knocked through the 49-yard winner to put Chicago within a game of the Super Bowl. "It's like a monkey off our back," Brian Urlacher said. "That was a good big kick—bad field, 49 yards, windy. That's why he's first-team All-Pro."

Fresh from their win over Seattle, the Bears were pitted against the New Orleans Saints in the NFC championship game on January 21, 2007, at Soldier Field. The Bears took an 18–14 lead into the fourth quarter when Grossman connected on four straight passes—the payoff was a 33-yarder to Bernard Berrian, which gave the Bears a 25–14 lead. Then the ground game took over. Cedric Benson scored on a 12-yard run, and Thomas Jones, who led the way with 123 yards, iced the super trip to Miami with a 15-yard run to cap the 39–14 victory. The Super Bowl matchup would pit two black coaches against one another—Tony Dungy for the Colts, Lovie Smith for Chicago—a first for the NFL. "I'm blessed," Smith said. "But I'll feel

The lions in front of the Art Institute of Chicago wear Bears helmets in support of the team's trip to Super Bowl XLI in 2007.

even better to be the first black coach to hold up the world championship trophy."

The Indianapolis Colts, though, had Peyton Manning calling the shots, and he was superb in every facet on that rain-swept evening. Manning countered Hester's opening kickoff return with a scoring pass to Reggie Wayne. Mixing his calls, Manning led the Colts to a 22–17 lead in the fourth quarter, when Kelvin Hayden intercepted Grossman and raced 56 yards down the sideline for the clincher. Indianapolis took Super Bowl XLI 29–17.

STARS OF THE ERA

Once again, after the lean decade of the '90s, the Bears began to assemble standout players to augment Brian Urlacher and spectacular kick returner Devin Hester.

Center **Olin Kreutz** was as steady, solid, and dependable as anyone in the decade. The 6'2", 292-pound Hawaiian center from the University of Washington came to the Bears in the third round of the 1998 draft. Completing his eleventh season in 2008, Kreutz always played—healthy or hurt. After being a reserve for most of 1998—his rookie year—he started the season finale and never looked back. Kreutz started all 16 games in a season eight times through 2008. He made the Pro Bowl each year from 2001 to 2006. And those six straight Pro Bowls tie him for fifth in team history, trailing only Walter Payton, Jay Hilgenberg, Stan Jones, and Mike Singletary. He made All-Pro first team in 2006.

Defense has been the foundation of the Bears in the recent memory of any league follower, dating back to George Allen's time as defensive coordinator in the early '60s. As fine a player as Urlacher has been, **Lance Briggs** has played at the same elite level and, in fact, was the only Bear in 2008 to be elected to the NFC Pro Bowl team. After wearing the franchise tag in 2007, Briggs finished his sixth Chicago season in 2008—a year that saw him sign a lucrative six-year contract extension, making him a Bear through the 2013 season. Briggs was a third-round draft choice in 2003, after three All-Pac-10 seasons at the University

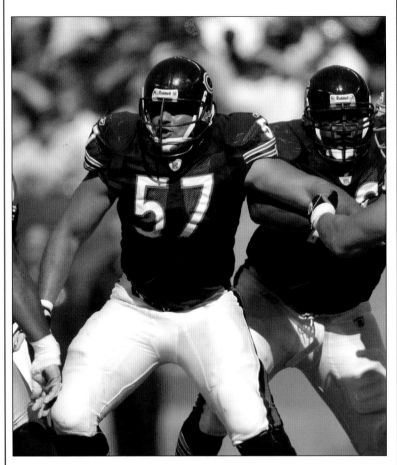

Since his 1998 arrival as a third-round draft pick from Washington, Honolulu native Olin Kreutz has supplied the "Hawaiian Punch" as anchor of the offensive line. A six-time Pro Bowler, Kreutz is the latest great Bear center.

Blood, sweat, and mud are all in a day's work for supreme outside linebacker Lance Briggs, whose stellar play has earned him four Pro Bowl appearances since he joined the team in the third round of the 2003 draft.

of Arizona. He became a starter at strong side linebacker in the fourth game that season and then moved to the weak side position the next season. He had returned three interceptions for touchdowns in his career through 2008 and was named to the All-Pro first team in 2005 and second team in 2006.

Mike Brown was selected from the University of Nebraska in the second round of the 2000 draft. A business major and three-year starter for the Huskers, Brown was named a first-team All-America safety in 1999 by the Associated Press and Football Writers of America, as well as a unanimous All-Big 12 selection and an academic All-American. Brown started as a rookie in 2000 and was named to several all-rookie teams. In 2001, Brown was an All-Pro first teamer in a season that saw him make five interceptions and earn NFC Player of the Week honors against the Lions on December 2, when he had nine tackles—including two sacks—and forced and recovered a fumble. His shining moments in team and league history came at midseason, when he became the first NFL player to end back-to-back overtime games (against the 49ers and the Browns) with interception returns for game-winning touchdowns. Brown's desire and intelligence are unquestioned, and he is regarded as a prime head-coaching prospect when he retires—if he chooses to remain in football.

Other notable players of the decade include running back **Thomas Jones,** who came to Chicago as a free agent in 2004 and led the Bears in rushing each of

Mike Brown gave the Bears nine marvelous seasons as a premier safety. He joined the team in 2000 as a second-round draft choice from Nebraska and was named to the All-Pro first team in 2001 after making five interceptions—two for game-winning, overtime touchdowns.

the three years he was with the team. Plus, his work ethic and personal values were unmatched. Very few players in team history have enjoyed the respect his teammates granted him.

Tommie Harris was the top draft choice of 2004, out of the University of Oklahoma, and was regarded as a top defensive tackle in the league until he hurt his knee in 2007. Extremely quick and strong, Harris was a force in 2008. He was named to Pro Bowls in 2005, 2006, and 2007 and was second team All-Pro in 2005 and 2006.

Defensive tackle Tommie Harris was the first player drafted at the beginning of the Lovie Smith era in 2004. The big playmaker was chosen for three consecutive NFL Pro Bowl teams. He joined the Bears after an All-America career at Oklahoma.

Quarterback remains the Bears' most unsettled position. It's not as though the Bears have been lacking; great names such as Johnny Lujack, George Blanda, Ed Brown, Billy Wade, and Jim McMahon have had big moments for the Bears. Rex Grossman, a fine long passer, quarterbacked the Bears to Super Bowl XLI. Kyle Orton led the Bears to the playoffs in both 2005 and again in 2008. But something has always gone wrong since Sid Luckman, the first T formation quarterback, retired in 1950—this position is star-crossed.

THE LETDOWN

igh hopes for a return to the Super Bowl in the 2007 season never materialized—the team couldn't get into synch. A record of 7–9 was a drastic comedown from 13–3, and the very real opportunity to add a second Vince Lombardi Trophy to the Halas Hall hardware display was lost.

Trouble was hinted at in the spring when Lovie Smith fired his defensive coordinator, Ron Rivera, who was well respected by players. Smith was apparently upset that other teams kept calling the Bears for permission to talk with Rivera. Long-time loyalist Bob Babich was promoted to the position. Jerry Angelo made another decision that backfired—he traded

It was tough times for the Bears at Soldier Field on October 28, 2007. Running back Cedric Benson is brought to earth by a pride of angry Detroit Lions in a 16–7 Bears defeat. The Bears fell to 7–9 after the 2006 Super Bowl season.

well-regarded running back and team leader Thomas Jones to the New York Jets and turned the starting job over to the 2005 top draft choice, Cedric Benson. Benson had never been popular with fans or his teammates due to contract disputes that caused him to miss most of the 2005 training camp.

The opener in San Diego between the two preseason Super Bowl favorites, the Bears and Chargers, turned out to be a defensive struggle, with the Chargers prevailing 14–3. After they beat the Kansas City Chiefs at Soldier Field, the Bears lost a pair of games to the Dallas Cowboys and Detroit Lions before they rebounded with a 27–20 win at Green Bay behind Brian Griese, who took over as quarterback after Rex Grossman was benched.

The Bears lurched along with off-and-on performances until late December in a campaign that saw them lose to both the Vikings and Lions, blow a 16–14 lead at home in a 21–16 loss to the fast-rising New York Giants, and then falter in Washington.

The brightest moments came from the ongoing excellence of Devin Hester. Hester ran back one kickoff at Detroit and one at home against Denver, as well as punts against Kansas City, Minnesota, Denver, and New Orleans.

Another promising performance came late in the season when Lovie Smith and offensive coordinator Ron Turner turned over quarterbacking duties to Kyle Orton. Orton was assertive in a 20–13 loss at Minnesota, a 35–7 rout of the Packers, and a 33–25 victory against the Saints in the season finale.

These were hard times. The defense had dropped from the NFL's upper levels to the bottom in total yards, rushing, and passing yardage allowed. The offense fared little better: 27th in total yards, 30th in rushing yards, and 15th in passing. Benson was a bust as a starter and would face rookie competition in the spring. How he responded to the challenge said as much about the man as it did about those who put their faith in him.

BEARS OFF THE FIELD

The Chicago Bears have long been enthusiastic participants in the National Football League's various charitable and community-relations programs that the late commissioner Pete Rozelle started in 1963. Two major programs the franchise heavily promotes are Bears Care and Bears Outreach.

Bears Care's mission is to support programs that target education, youth athletics, medical research, and health awareness. The main medical research programs focus on breast cancer and ovarian cancer. Bears players and staff members have generously given their time to participate in various activities. By involving area businesses and organizations, as well as individual donors, Bears Care—since its incorporation in 2005 as a 501(d)3 organization—has issued grants totaling more than $3 million to more than 40 qualifying agencies, impacting thousands of Chicago-area individuals and families each year.

Bears Outreach covers at least 18 areas of community programs, initiatives, and partnerships. Perhaps the best known is the team's annual Brian Piccolo Award, honoring a veteran and rookie each year who exemplifies Piccolo's courage, loyalty, teamwork, dedication, and sense of humor.

In addition to the aforementioned programs, each Tuesday during the football season, Bears players visit schools to speak to students, share their own experiences, and provide motivation. They have direct contact with at least 7,000 students each fall. The Bears honor a High School Coach of the Week all season, and the team has made donations for new football fields to several high schools.

In recognition of player outreach, the NFL's most prestigious individual honor that recognizes a player for his activities off the field and in his community, as well as on-field excellence, is the Walter Payton Man of the Year Award, named for the Hall of Famer after his death in 1999. Man of the Year began in 1970 in order to honor the player who best balances his civic and professional responsibilities. Bears who have won this award include running back Walter Payton in 1977; safety Dave Duerson in 1987; middle linebacker Mike Singletary in 1990; and defensive tackle Jim Flanigan, a 2000 co-winner. And Bears players don't just receive awards—they also nominate candidates for NFL Teacher of the Year to honor an individual who made a difference in their lives.

Chicago Bear Israel Idonije (right) takes part in an NFL Players Clinic with Special Olympic athletes in Washington, D.C., in 2008. Reaching out to others is an important part of a player's life.

FOLLOWING THE BEARS

Non-stop interest in the Bears was triggered by the incredible success of the 1985 Super Bowl season, which spawned blanket coverage by the four television stations—all running nightly newscasts in Chicago—plus several radio stations. All-sports radio did not come to Chicago until the '90s; it was similar with sports television. Thus, the stations that were doing newscasts then—WBBM-TV 2, WMAQ-TV 5, WLS-TV 7, and WGN-TV 9—had to compete for every story and go out of their way to find their own angles while they schemed to outmaneuver the newspapers in three- to four-minute chunks. With names such as Johnny Morris, Chet Coppock, Mark Giangreco, and Tim Weigel out front, plus their producers seeking inside edges every day, competition was tough, fair, fun…and wonderful.

Today, in the era of the 24/7 news cycle, there's no way a fan can be starved for info about the Bears. It's simply unavoidable, no matter the medium. The area newspapers, radio and cable stations, specialty magazines, and Internet outlets constantly feed fan interest and informational needs outside the game-day network telecasts and local radio broadcasts (currently on WBBM 780-AM).

In 1941, the Bears became the first pro football team to air their games on the radio, with Bert Wilson handling play-by-play on WIND. Since then, such voices as Jack Brickhouse, Irv Kupcinet, Joe McConnell, Brad Palmer, Wayne Larrivee, Hub Arkush, and Gary Bender have called the games on WGN, WMAQ, and WBBM. Play-by-play man Jeff Joniak currently has the call and is joined by former Bears offensive lineman Tom Thayer, who provides the color. The Joniak-Thayer combination is heard on 28 radio network stations in Illinois, Indiana, and Iowa, as well as in Nevada on KSHP-Las Vegas.

On *Bears Insider,* a live radio broadcast on Monday nights, head coach Lovie Smith answers calls and e-mails from Bears fans. Online, ChicagoBears.com is the team's official website, which includes special features, practice reports, and videos of player interviews.

FOX Chicago carries the team's preseason telecasts on a seven-station network in Illinois, Iowa, and northern Indiana. On Sunday mornings, whether the Bears play or not that day, FOX Chicago carries a lineup that includes *FOX Kickoff Sunday, Bears Gameday Live,* and *FOX NFL Sunday.* On Sunday night, FOX carries *Bears Gamenight Live,* a postgame wrap-up program that includes an exclusive interview with coach Smith following the station's newscast.

Meanwhile, Comcast SportsNet Chicago carries *Bears Blitz,* an informational program on Wednesday and Thursday nights that covers the team from all angles—from highlights to press conferences to player interviews.

Jeff Joniak of WBBM has been the Bears' radio play-by-play announcer since 1997. Joniak follows a tradition started by Bert Wilson in 1941 and continued by Jack Brickhouse, Joe McConnell, Wayne Larrivee, and Gary Bender.

A statue of Jack Brickhouse stands at the WGN radio studio in Chicago, Illinois. The voice of the Cubs on WGN-TV from 1948 to 1981, Brickhouse also called Bears games on WGN Radio from 1953 to 1976.

MEDIOCRITY DOESN'T CUT IT

The Chicago Bears of 2008 finished out of the playoffs at 9–7; it was a lackluster display of football. They bagged a couple of unexpected victories. One win came in the opener at Indianapolis. Three weeks later, at home against Philadelphia, the Bears unleashed a game-saving, goal-line stand that preserved a 24–20 win.

All that fell by the wayside, though, as the team could only offer the running of rookie Matt Forte to counterbalance the least-impressive receiving corps in the league—and it only made Kyle Orton's job that much harder. This deficiency became evident when receivers deemed unworthy in Chicago—such as Bernard Berrian and Bobby Wade in Minnesota and Justin Gage in Tennessee—excelled in enemy uniforms.

Defense—the hallmark of the Bears' championship teams of '63 and '85, along with the 2006 Super Bowl year—turned passive under the Cover 2 system of coach Lovie Smith and his friend and handpicked defensive coordinator, Bob Babich. A nonexistent pass rush and porous pass coverage, especially in third-and-long situations, cost the Bears three early-season, last-second defeats to Carolina, Tampa Bay in overtime, and Atlanta.

The team got pushed around shamelessly on the road against Green Bay on November 16 and two weeks later at Minnesota. In the process, they lost control of a weak and easily winnable NFC North Division and had to scramble to stay alive in the last month. They still had a chance to make the playoffs on the final Sunday with a win but lost out—the Houston Texans ran up 455 yards in a 31–24 victory.

Smith tried to put a positive spin on the 2008 Bears. "We're close," Smith said after the final defeat in a season of frustrating losses. Few were buying Smith's line—not even his boss, GM Jerry Angelo, who admitted the team needed to find a franchise quarterback. "That's the key," Angelo said in his seasonal postmortem.

In April 2009, Angelo backed up his words by acquiring quarterback Jay Cutler from the Denver Broncos. Cutler came at a price—the Bears gave up their 2009 and 2010 first-round draft picks and Orton as part of the trade—but he possesses the arm strength and mobility that the Bears have been sorely lacking at quarterback. His addition represents a bold step into the future for the Monsters of the Midway—one of the NFL's flagship franchises.

By the preseason opener at Arrowhead Stadium in Kansas City on August 7, second-round choice Matt Forte (22) showed the right stuff. Forte ran for 1,231 yards and caught 64 passes for 484 more. He scored 12 touchdowns.

THE BEARS ACQUIRE CUTLER

On April 2, 2009, in what some Bears observers have called the biggest move in franchise history, the Bears acquired 25-year-old Jay Cutler in a trade. Named to the Pro Bowl in only his third NFL season in 2008, Cutler told the media, "I don't see myself as the savior" but added, "I am a Chicago Bear, and I am happy to be here."

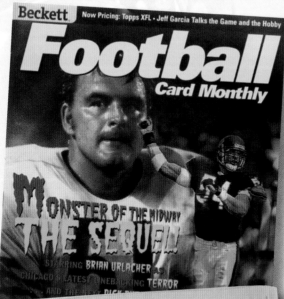

Bears middle linebacker Brian Urlacher stars as "Chicago's Latest Linebacking Terror" on the cover of Beckett Football Card Monthly in May 2001.

The Bears' 2007 trip to south Florida for Super Bowl XLI is worthy of a commemorative pin.

In December 2006, the Chicago Tribune details the sad case of troubled defensive tackle Tank Johnson.

A Bear claw is just another way for fans to express their loyalty to the team they support.

With arms raised in victory, this program foreshadows the Bears' win over the New Orleans Saints, 39-14, in the 2007 NFC championship game. The Bears advanced to Super Bowl XLI.

This Bears pennant spells out the 2005-06 success story for the Bears, the NFC North champions.

Much like the player himself, Devin Hester's bobblehead can't stand still—he's immortalized while making a play.

The *Chicago Sun-Times's* front-page story gives the Bears advice on how to deal with the Colts in Super Bowl XLI.

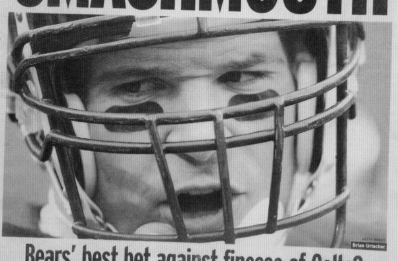

DEVIN HESTER

BEARS BY THE NUMBERS

SEASON RECORDS, 1920–2008

Year	Coach	Record	Result/Remarks/Postseason
1920	G. S. Halas/E. Sternaman	10–1–2	2nd as Decatur Staleys
1921	Halas/Sternaman	9–1–1	APFA/Title #1 as Chicago Staleys
1922	Halas/Sternaman	9–3	2nd as Chicago Bears/NFL
1923	Halas/Sternaman	9–2–1	2nd
1924	Halas/Sternaman	6–1–4	2nd
1925	Halas/Sternaman	9–5–3	7th/Grange Tour
1926	Halas/Sternaman	12–1–3	2nd
1927	Halas/Sternaman	9–3–2	3rd
1928	Halas/Sternaman	7–5–1	5th
1929	Halas/Sternaman	4–9–2	9th
1930	Ralph Jones	9–4–1	3rd
1931	Ralph Jones	8–5	3rd
1932	Ralph Jones	7–1–6	1st/Title #2
1933	George Halas	10–2–1	1 West/Beat NY Giants 23–21, Title #3
1934	George Halas	13–0	1 West/Lost to NY Giants 30–13 for title
1935	George Halas	6–4–2	3 West
1936	George Halas	9–3	2 West
1937	George Halas	9–1–1	1 West/Lost to Washington 28–21 for title
1938	George Halas	6–5	3 West
1939	George Halas	8–3	2 West
1940	George Halas	8–3	1 West/Beat Washington 73–0, Title #4
1941	George Halas	10–1	1 West/Beat Green Bay 33–14 playoff/ Beat NY Giants 37–9, Title #5
1942	Halas/Anderson/Johnsos	11–0	1 West/Lost title to Washington 14–6
1943	Anderson/Johnsos	8–1–1	1 West/Beat Washington 41–21, Title #6

Year	Coach	Record	Result/Remarks/Postseason
1944	Anderson/Johnsos	6–3–1	2 West
1945	Anderson/Johnsos	3–7	4 West
1946	George Halas	8–2–1	1 West/Beat NY Giants 24–14, Title #7
1947	George Halas	8–4	2 West
1948	George Halas	10–2	2 West
1949	George Halas	9–3	2 West
1950	George Halas	9–3	T1 Natl/Lost playoff to LA Rams 24–14
1951	George Halas	7–5	4 Natl
1952	George Halas	5–7	5 Natl
1953	George Halas	3–8–1	4 West
1954	George Halas	8–4	2 West
1955	George Halas	8–4	2 West
1956	Paddy Driscoll	9–2–1	1 West/Lost to NY Giants 47–7 for title
1957	Paddy Driscoll	5–7	5 West
1958	George Halas	8–4	2 West
1959	George Halas	8–4	2 West
1960	George Halas	5–6–1	5 West
1961	George Halas	8–6	T3 West
1962	George Halas	9–5	3 West
1963	George Halas	11–1–2	1 West/Beat NY Giants 14–10, Title #8
1964	George Halas	5–9	6 West
1965	George Halas	9–5	3 West
1966	George Halas	5–7–2	5 West
1967	George Halas	7–6–1	2 Central
1968	Jim Dooley	7–7	2 Central
1969	Jim Dooley	1–13	4 Central
1970	Jim Dooley	6–8	3 NFC Central

Year	Coach	Record	Result/Remarks/Postseason
1971	Jim Dooley	6–8	3 NFC Central
1972	Abe Gibron	4–9–1	4 NFC Central
1973	Abe Gibron	3–11	4 NFC Central
1974	Abe Gibron	4–10	4 NFC Central
1975	Jack Pardee	4–10	T3 NFC Central
1976	Jack Pardee	7–7	2 NFC Central
1977	Jack Pardee	9–5	2 NFC Central/Lost WC to Dallas 37–7
1978	Neill Armstrong	7–9	T3 NFC Central
1979	Neill Armstrong	10–6	2 NFC Central/Lost WC to Philadelphia 27–17
1980	Neill Armstrong	7–9	3 NFC Central
1981	Neill Armstrong	6–10	5 NFC Central
1982	Mike Ditka	3–6	12 NFC/Strike-shortened season
1983	Mike Ditka	8–8	3 NFC Central/Halas dies 10/31
1984	Mike Ditka	10–6	1 NFC Central/Beat Washington 23–19/Lost NFC title to SF 23–0
1985	Mike Ditka	15–1	1 NFC Central/Beat NY Giants 21–0/ LA Rams 24–0 NFC/New England 46–10 SB XX, Title #9
1986	Mike Ditka	14–2	1 NFC Central/Lost playoff to Washington 27–13
1987	Mike Ditka	11–4	1 NFC Central/Lost playoff to Washington 21–17
1988	Mike Ditka	12–4	1 NFC Central/Beat Philadelphia 20–12/Lost NFC divisional to SF 28–3
1989	Mike Ditka	6–10	4 NFC Central
1990	Mike Ditka	11–5	1 NFC Central/Beat New Orleans 16–6/Lost NFC title to NY Giants 31–3
1991	Mike Ditka	11–5	2 NFC Central/Lost to Dallas 17–13
1992	Mike Ditka	5–11	T3 NFC Central
1993	Dave Wannstedt	7–9	4 NFC Central
1994	Dave Wannstedt	9–7	T2 NFC Central/Beat Minnesota 35–18/Lost to SF 44–15
1995	Dave Wannstedt	9–7	3 NFC Central
1996	Dave Wannstedt	7–9	3 NFC Central
1997	Dave Wannstedt	4–12	4 NFC Central
1998	Dave Wannstedt	4–12	4 NFC Central
1999	Dick Jauron	6–10	4 NFC Central
2000	Dick Jauron	5–11	5 NFC Central
2001	Dick Jauron	13–3	1 NFC Central/Lost to Philadelphia 33–19
2002	Dick Jauron	4–12	3 NFC North
2003	Dick Jauron	7–9	3 NFC North
2004	Lovie Smith	5–11	4 NFC North
2005	Lovie Smith	11–5	1 NFC North/Lost to Carolina 29–21
2006	Lovie Smith	13–3	1 NFC North/Beat Seattle 27–24 OT/ Beat New Orleans 39–14 NFC/Lost SB XLI to Indianapolis 29–17
2007	Lovie Smith	7–9	4 NFC North
2008	Lovie Smith	9–7	2 NFC North

HEAD COACHES

Coach	Seasons	Overall	Regular	Postseason
George Halas	1920–29 1932–42 1946–55 1958–67	324–151–31	318–148–31	6–3/6 titles
(Ed Sternaman Co-coach with Halas 1920–29: 84–31–19)				
Ralph Jones	1930–32	24–10–7	24–10–7	0–0/1 title
Hunk Anderson & Luke Johnsos	1942–45	24–12–2	23–11–2	1–1/1 title
John "Paddy" Driscoll	1956–57	14–10–1	14–9–1	0–1
Jim Dooley	1968–71	20–36–0	20–36–0	None
Abe Gibron	1972–74	11–30–1	11–30–1	None
Jack Pardee	1975–77	20–23–0	20–22–0	0–1
Neill Armstrong	1978–81	30–35–0	30–34–0	0–1
Mike Ditka	1982–92	112–68–0	106–62–0	6–6/1 title
Dave Wannstedt	1993–98	41–57–0	40–56–0	1–1

Coach	Seasons	Overall	Regular	Postseason
Dick Jauron	1999–2003	35–46–0	35–45–0	0–1
Lovie Smith	2004–Present	47–37–0	45–35–0	2–2

PLAYOFF GAME RESULTS

Date	Game	Winner	Loser	Score	Site
12–17–33	NFL Championship	BEARS	NY Giants	23–21	Wrigley Field
12–09–34	NFL Championship	NY Giants	BEARS	30–13	Polo Grounds
12–12–37	NFL Championship	Washington	BEARS	28–21	Wrigley Field
12–08–40	NFL Championship	BEARS	Washington	73–0	Griffith Stadium
12–14–41	West Championship	BEARS	Green Bay	33–14	Wrigley Field
12–21–41	NFL Championship	BEARS	NY Giants	37–9	Wrigley Field
12–13–42	NFL Championship	Washington	BEARS	14–6	Griffith Stadium
12–26–43	NFL Championship	BEARS	Washington	41–21	Wrigley Field
12–15–46	NFL Championship	BEARS	NY Giants	24–14	Polo Grounds
12–17–50	West Championship	LA Rams	BEARS	24–14	LA Coliseum
12–30–56	NFL Championship	NY Giants	BEARS	47–7	Yankee Stadium
12–29–63	NFL Championship	BEARS	NY Giants	14–10	Wrigley Field
12–26–77	NFC Divisional	Dallas	BEARS	37–7	Texas Stadium
12–23–79	NFC Divisional	Philadelphia	BEARS	27–7	Veterans Stadium
12–30–84	NFC Divisional	BEARS	Washington	23–19	RFK Stadium
01–06–85	NFC Championship	San Francisco	BEARS	23–0	Candlestick Park
01–05–86	NFC Divisional	BEARS	NY Giants	21–0	Soldier Field
01–12–86	NFC Championship	BEARS	LA Rams	24–0	Soldier Field
01–26–86	Super Bowl XX	BEARS	New England	46–10	Louisiana Superdome
01–03–87	NFC Divisional	Washington	BEARS	27–13	Soldier Field
01–10–88	NFC Divisional	Washington	BEARS	21–17	Soldier Field
12–31–88	NFC Divisional	BEARS	Philadelphia	20–12	Soldier Field
01–08–89	NFC Championship	San Francisco	BEARS	28–3	Soldier Field
01–06–91	NFC Divisional	BEARS	New Orleans	16–6	Soldier Field
01–13–91	NFC Divisional	NY Giants	BEARS	31–3	Giants Stadium
12–29–91	NFC First Round	Dallas	BEARS	17–13	Soldier Field
01–01–95	NFC First Round	BEARS	Minnesota	35–18	Metrodome
01–07–95	NFC Divisional	San Francisco	BEARS	44–15	Candlestick Park
01–19–02	NFC Divisional	Philadelphia	BEARS	33–19	Soldier Field
01–15–06	NFC Divisional	Carolina	BEARS	29–21	Soldier Field
01–14–07	NFC Divisional	BEARS	Seattle	27–24	(OT) Soldier Field
01–21–07	NFC Championship	BEARS	New Orleans	39–14	Soldier Field
02–04–07	Super Bowl XLI	Indianapolis	BEARS	29–17	Dolphins Stadium

BEARS IN THE PRO FOOTBALL HALL OF FAME

Name & No.	Position	Inducted	Total Seasons with Bears	NFL
George Halas #7	Owner-Coach-End	1963	63 (1920–83)	63
Harold "Red" Grange #77	Halfback, DB	1963	7 (1925, 29–34)	9
Bronko Nagurski #3	Fullback, Tackle	1963	9 (1930–37, 43)	9
George Trafton #13	Center	1964	13 (1920–32)	13
Ed Healey #16	Tackle	1964	6 (1922–27)	8
Roy "Link" Lyman #2,11	Tackle	1964	7 (1926–34)	11
Sid Luckman #42	Quarterback	1965	12 (1939–50)	12
Danny Fortmann #21	Guard	1965	8 (1936–43)	8
John "Paddy" Driscoll #1	Halfback	1965	5 (1920, 26–29)	10
George McAfee #5	Halfback, DB	1966	8 (1940–41, 45–50)	8
Clyde "Bulldog" Turner #66	Center, Linebacker	1966	13 (1940–52)	13
Joe Stydahar #13	Tackle	1967	9 (1936–42, 45–46)	9
Bill Hewitt #56	End	1971	5 (1932–36)	9
Bill George #61	Linebacker	1974	14 (1952–65)	15
George Connor #71	Linebacker, Tackle	1975	8 (1948–55)	8
Gale Sayers #40	Running Back	1977	7 (1965–71)	7
Dick Butkus #51	Linebacker	1979	9 (1965–73)	9
George Blanda #16	Quarterback, Kicker	1981	10 (1949–58)	26
Doug Atkins #81	Defensive End	1982	12 (1955–66)	17
George Musso #16	Tackle, Guard	1982	12 (1933–44)	12
Mike Ditka #89	Tight End, Coach	1988	17 Player (1961–66) Coach (1982–92)	34
Stan Jones #78	Guard, Def. Tackle	1991	12 (1954–65)	13
Walter Payton #34	Running Back	1993	13 (1975–87)	13
Jim Finks	VP & Gen. Mgr.	1995	9 (1974–82)	34
Mike Singletary #50	Linebacker	1998	12 (1981–92)	12
Dan Hampton #99	Def. End, Tackle	2002	12 (1979–90)	12

Hall of Famers who played briefly for the Bears: Jimmy Conzelman (1920), Guy Chamberlain (1921), Walt Kieseling (1934), Bobby Layne (1948), Alan Page (1978–81)

RETIRED NUMBERS

3	Bronko Nagurski, Fullback, Tackle
5	George McAfee, Halfback
7	George Halas, End
28	Willie Galimore, Running Back
34	Walter Payton, Running Back
40	Gale Sayers, Running Back
41	Brian Piccolo, Running Back
42	Sid Luckman, Quarterback
51	Dick Butkus, Linebacker
56	Bill Hewitt, End
61	Bill George, Linebacker
66	Clyde "Bulldog" Turner, Center
77	Harold "Red" Grange, Halfback

Walter Payton used this helmet from 1975 to 1987 with the Chicago Bears.

NFL AWARD WINNERS

NFL WALTER PAYTON MAN OF THE YEAR

1977	Walter Payton, Running Back
1987	Dave Duerson, Safety
1990	Mike Singletary, Linebacker
2000	Jim Flanigan, Defensive Tackle (Cowinner)

NFL MOST VALUABLE PLAYER

1943	Sid Luckman, Quarterback, Joe Carr Trophy
1955	Harlon Hill, End, Jim Thorpe Trophy
1977	Walter Payton, Running Back, AP, PFWA
1985	Walter Payton, Running Back, Newspaper Enterprise Association NFL MVP Award

PLAYER OF THE YEAR

1977	Walter Payton, Running Back, NFC/AP Offense, NFC/UPI Offense
1985	Walter Payton, Running Back, NFC/UPI Offense
1985	Mike Singletary, Linebacker, AP Defense, NFC/UPI Defense
1988	Mike Singletary, Linebacker, AP Defense, NFC/UPI Defense
2005	Brian Urlacher, Linebacker, AP Defense

ROOKIE OF THE YEAR

1961	Mike Ditka, Tight End, NFL/UPI
1962	Ronnie Bull, Running Back, NFL/UPI
1965	Gale Sayers, Running Back, NFL/UPI
1973	Wally Chambers, Defensive End, AP Defense
1982	Jim McMahon, Quarterback, NFL/UPI
1990	Mark Carrier, Safety, NFL/UPI, NFL/AP Defense
1995	Rashaan Salaam, Running Back, NFL/UPI
2000	Brian Urlacher, Linebacker, NFL/AP Defense
2001	Anthony Thomas, Running Back, NFL/AP Offense

COACH OF THE YEAR (NFL OR NFC)

George Halas	1963, 1965
Mike Ditka	1985, 1988
Dave Wannstedt	1994
Dick Jauron	2001
Lovie Smith	2005

TEAM RECORDS/STATISTICAL LEADERS
(*NFL RECORD, **TIED NFL RECORD)

SERVICE

Seasons	14	Doug Buffone, 1966–79
	14	Bill George, 1952–65
Games	191	Steve McMichael, 1981–93
Starts	184	Walter Payton, 1975–87
Consecutive Games	191	Steve McMichael, 1981–93
Pro Bowls	10	Mike Singletary, 1984–93

SCORING (POINTS)

Game	36	Gale Sayers, vs. SF 12/12/65 (6 TDs)
Consecutive Games	83	George Blanda, 10/28/51–11/9/58
Season	144	Kevin Butler, 1985 (51 XP, 31 FG)
Career	1,116	Kevin Butler, 1985–95 (387 XP, 243 FG)

TOUCHDOWNS (RUSHES, RECEPTIONS, RETURNS)

Game	6**	Gale Sayers, vs. SF 12/12/65 (4–1–1)
Consecutive Games	8	Rick Casares, 11/59–9/25/60
Season	22	Gale Sayers, 1965
Career	125	Walter Payton, 1975–87 (110–15–0)

SAFETIES

| Career | 3 | Steve McMichael, 1981–93 |

RUSHING

RUSHING ATTEMPTS

Game	40	Walter Payton, vs. MIN 11/20/77 (275 yards)
Season	381	Walter Payton, 1984
Career	3,838	Walter Payton, 1975–87

RUSHING YARDS

Game	275	Walter Payton, vs. MIN 11/20/77
Season	1,852	Walter Payton, 1977
Career	16,726	Walter Payton, 1975–87

GAMES RUSHING FOR 100 YARDS OR MORE

Season	10	Walter Payton, 1977, 1985
Career	77	Walter Payton, 1975–87
Consecutive Games	10	Walter Payton, 10/13–12/8/85

RUSHING TOUCHDOWNS

Game	4	Bobby Douglass, at GB 11/4/73
	4	Gale Sayers, vs. SF 12/12/65
	4	Rick Casares, vs. PIT 12/6/59, at SF 10/28/56
Consecutive Games	7	Walter Payton, 10/3–11/14/76
	7	Gale Sayers, 10/26–12/6/69
Season	14	Walter Payton, 1977, 1979
	14	Gale Sayers, 1965
Career	110	Walter Payton, 1975–87

PASSING

QB RATING
Season (100+ attempts)	107.8	Sid Luckman, 1943
Career (400+ attempts)	80.7	Erik Kramer, 1994–98

PASS ATTEMPTS
Game	60	Erik Kramer, vs. NYJ 11/16/97
Season	522	Erik Kramer, 1995
Career	1,759	Jim Harbaugh, 1987–93

COMPLETIONS
Game	34	Brian Griese, at DET 9/30/07
	34	Jim Miller, vs. MIN 11/14/99
Consecutive Games	15	Shane Matthews, vs. NE 12/10/00
Season	315	Erik Kramer, 1995
Career	1,023	Jim Harbaugh, 1987–93
Long	98	Bill Wade, at DET 10/8/61 TD to John Farrington

PASSING YARDS
Game	468	Johnny Lujack, vs. CHI Cards 12/11/49
Season	3,838	Erik Kramer, 1995
Career	14,686	Sid Luckman, 1939–50

300-YARD GAMES
Season	4	Bill Wade, 1962
Consecutive Games	2	Brian Griese, 10/14–10/21/2007
	2	Jim Miller, 11/14–11/21/99
	2	Bill Wade, 10/14–10/21/62, 11/18–11/25/62
	2	George Blanda, 10/17–10/24/54
	2	Sid Luckman, 10/12–10/19/47
Career	9	Bill Wade, 1961–66

TOUCHDOWN PASSES
Game	7	Sid Luckman, at NYG 11/14/43*
Consecutive Games	19	Sid Luckman, 11/22/42–11/26/44
Season	29	Erik Kramer, 1995
Career	137	Sid Luckman, 1939–50

RECEIVING

RECEPTIONS
Game	14	Jim Keane, at NYG 10/23/49
Consecutive Games	58	Marty Booker, 9/24/00–12/28/2003
Season	100	Marty Booker, 2001
Career	492	Walter Payton, 1975–87

YARDS
Game	214	Harlon Hill, at SF 10/31/54
Season	1,400	Marcus Robinson, 1999
Career	5,059	Johnny Morris, 1958–67
Long	98	John Farrington, TD 10/8/61

TOUCHDOWNS
Game	4	Mike Ditka, vs. LA Rams 10/13/63
	4	Harlon Hill, vs. SF 10/31/54
Consecutive Games	7	Curtis Conway, 9/24–11/12/95
	7	Ken Kavanaugh, 11/2–12/14/47
Season	13	Dick Gordon, 1970
	13	Ken Kavanaugh, 1947
Career	50	Ken Kavanaugh, 1940–41, 1945–50

INTERCEPTING

INTERCEPTIONS
Game	3	Mark Carrier, at WASH 12/9/90
	3	Ross Brupbacher, vs. DEN 12/12/76
	3	Curtis Gentry, vs. STL Cards 11/19/67
	3	Richie Petitbon, at GB 9/24/67
	3	Johnny Lujack, at GB 9/26/48
	3	Bob Margarita, vs. DET 11/11/45
Consecutive Games	4	LAST: Dave Duerson, 9/14–10/5/86
Season	10	Mark Carrier, 1990
Career	38	Gary Fencik, 1976–87

TOUCHDOWNS

Game	1	LAST: Charles Tillman, at DET 10/5/2008
Season	2	LAST: Mike Brown, 2001
Career	4	Mike Brown, 2000–08
	4	Bennie McRae, 1962–70

PUNTING

PUNTS

Game	14	Keith Molesworth, vs. GB 12/10/33
Season	114**	Bob Parsons, 1981
Career	884	Bob Parsons, 1972–83

GROSS AVERAGE

Game (4+ punts)	57.3	Fred (Curly) Morrison, vs. LA Rams 11/16/52
Season (30+ punts)	46.5	Bobby Joe Green, 1963
Career (75+ punts)	44.5	George Gulyanics, 1947–52

PUNT RETURNS

RETURNS

Game	8	Jeff Fisher, at DET 12/16/84
Season	58	Jeff Fisher, 1984
Career	127	Dennis McKinnon, 1983–85, 1987–89

YARDS

Game	152	Devin Hester, at AZ 10/16/06
Long	95	Johnny Bailey (TD), vs. KC 12/29/90
Season	651	Devin Hester, 2007
Career	1,449	Devin Hester, 2006–08

AVERAGE

Game (3+ returns)	36.0	George McAfee, vs. LA Rams 10/10/48
Season (15+ returns)	15.5	Devin Hester, 2007
Career (50+ returns)	14.1*	Devin Hester, 2006–08

TOUCHDOWNS

Game	1	LAST: Devin Hester, vs. NO 12/30/07
Season	4**	Devin Hester, 2007
Career	7	Devin Hester, 2006–08

KICKOFF RETURNS

RETURNS

Game	9	Ahmad Merritt, at SF 9//07/03
Season	63	Glyn Milburn, 2000
Career	192	Glyn Milburn, 1998–2001

YARDS

Long	103	Gale Sayers, at PIT 9/17/67
Season	1,550	Glyn Milburn, 1998
Career	4,596	Glyn Milburn, 1998–2001

AVERAGE

Game (3+ returns)	56.3	Devin Hester, at STL Rams 12/11/06
Season (1+ per game)	37.7	Gale Sayers, 1967
Career (50+ returns)	30.6	Gale Sayers, 1965–71

TOUCHDOWNS

Game	2**	Devin Hester, at STL Rams 12/11/06
Season	4**	Cecil Turner, 1970
Career	6**	Gale Sayers, 1965–71

The 1985 Super Bowl Greats include Jim McMahon, Walter Payton, Mike Singletary, and Dan Hampton.

INDEX

This drawing shows George Halas as a player and a coach for the Bears.